PostgreSQL 16 Cookbook

Second Edition

AF668147

Solve challenges across scalability, performance optimization, essential commands, cloud provisioning, backup, and recovery

Peter G

Copyright © 2024 by GitforGits

All rights reserved. This book is protected under copyright laws and no part of it may be reproduced or transmitted in any form or by any means, electronic or mechanical, including photocopying, recording, or by any information storage and retrieval system, without the prior written permission of the publisher. Any unauthorized reproduction, distribution, or transmission of this work may result in civil and criminal penalties and will be dealt with in the respective jurisdiction at anywhere in India, in accordance with the applicable copyright laws.

Published by: GitforGits

Publisher: Sonal Dhandre

www.gitforgits.com

support@gitforgits.com

Printed in India

First Printing: August 2024

ISBN: 978-81-19177-50-9

Cover Design by: Kitten Publishing

For permission to use material from this book, please contact GitforGits at support@gitforgits.com.

Prologue

It is with great pleasure that I, as the author of "PostgreSQL 16 Cookbook, Second Edition," join you on such a journey of addressing PostgreSQL flaws. PostgreSQL has long been regarded as a pillar of the open-source database community, known for its robustness, scalability, and extensibility. My goals in revising this book for a second time are to make it more up-to-date with the features and improvements in PostgreSQL 16 and to fix any mistakes or missing information from the original so that it is useful for database administration novices and experts alike.

With great effort, I have integrated the new features and enhancements brought in by PostgreSQL 16, such as improved logical replication, which permits replication from standby servers. I explore these new possibilities for data availability and workload distribution in detail, giving you examples and solutions to help you implement them in your own environments. One of the most notable features of PostgreSQL 16 is the addition of SIMD acceleration, which significantly improves the performance of string processing tasks. I've dedicated an entire chapter to SIMD acceleration, demonstrating how to use this feature to optimize database operations, especially when dealing with large amounts of JSON and ASCII data. Through practical examples, I demonstrate the performance gains possible with SIMD, allowing you to maximize the potential of your hardware. I've expanded the security and access control sections to include enhancements, as well as tips for configuring user roles and privileges to effectively protect your data. This edition also covers advanced authentication methods like LDAP and SSL, giving you the knowledge you need to protect your databases from modern threats.

Along with these updates, I've fixed the problems with the previous edition by breaking down tricky concepts and giving more thorough explanations where they were lacking. For example, the backup and recovery sections have been thoroughly revised to include new tools such as pgBackRest and Barman, which provide powerful solutions for point-in-time recovery and continuous archiving. I've included practical examples to help you set up reliable backup strategies, ensuring that you're prepared for any situation. I've also worked on integrating PostgreSQL with modern programming languages, particularly Rust. Rust's growing popularity in the systems programming community makes it an excellent choice for developing high-performance database applications. I've included examples from popular Rust libraries such as pgx and rust-postgres that show how you can use Rust's safety and concurrency features to create efficient and dependable database applications.

My goal throughout this book is to give you a clear and practical understanding of PostgreSQL 16, allowing you to face the challenges of database management with confidence. Whether you're upgrading from PostgreSQL 15 or starting from scratch with version 16, this cookbook provides a wealth of information and insights to help you succeed. I've worked hard to make this second edition an indispensable resource for anyone working with PostgreSQL by filling in the gaps and inaccuracies of the previous edition and incorporating the most recent developments. Thank you for joining me on this journey, and I hope you find this edition useful and inspiring.

Content

Preface

Offering a detailed practical look at PostgreSQL 16's new features, "PostgreSQL 16 Cookbook, Second Edition" equips database administrators and developers to take advantage of the most recent developments. Building on the foundation of version 15, this second edition with version 16 walks you through the enhancements that make PostgreSQL a game changer in the database world.

This edition provides in-depth coverage of enhanced logical replication, which now includes the ability to replicate from standby servers. We provide detailed instructions for setting up these advanced replication configurations, allowing you to better distribute workloads and improve data availability. The optimization of concurrent bulk loading capabilities for faster data ingestion is another noteworthy addition. Another standout feature of PostgreSQL 16 is the expanded SQL/JSON syntax, which gives developers more control over JSON data management. Our book contains practical solutions and examples for using the new JSON functions and operators, which make it easier to store, query, and manipulate JSON data in your applications. We walk you through the process of configuring refined user roles and permissions, ensuring effective access control in complex environments. Additionally, the book teaches new monitoring capabilities introduced with the pg_stat_io view, which provide insights into I/O operations to help optimize performance.

The book goes on to implement performance enhancements such as SIMD acceleration for processing ASCII and JSON strings, as well as the new load balancing feature, load_balance_hosts, which distributes traffic efficiently among multiple servers. The goal of this book is to provide you with the knowledge you need to successfully manage, optimize, and troubleshoot database environments by providing a deep-dive understanding of how to implement and benefit from PostgreSQL 16's latest features.

In this book you will learn how to:

- Boost data availability and workload distribution using advanced logical replication techniques.
- Apply the SIMD acceleration to expedite the processing of ASCII and JSON strings.
- Make use of improved SQL/JSON syntax to manage complicated JSON data operations.
- Enhance efficiency and decrease query times by optimizing query performance with parallel execution.
- Utilize pg_stat_io for troubleshooting and monitoring I/O operations.
- Utilize Rust libraries like pgx and rust-postgres for easy integration with PostgreSQL.

- Distribute workload among numerous PostgreSQL instances by configuring load_balance_hosts.
- Simplify user role configurations and security with refined privilege management.
- Utilize pgBackRest and Barman to implement strong backup strategies.
- Optimize database performance using concurrent bulk loading.

GitforGits

Prerequisites

If you work with PostgreSQL and want to stay up to date on the latest advancements, debugging techniques, and database tricks, you've come to the right place. You will learn everything you need to know to become an expert database administrator from this book.

Codes Usage

Are you in need of some helpful code examples to assist you in your programming and documentation? Look no further! Our book offers a wealth of supplemental material, including code examples and exercises.

Not only is this book here to aid you in getting your job done, but you have our permission to use the example code in your programs and documentation. However, please note that if you are reproducing a significant portion of the code, we do require you to contact us for permission.

But don't worry, using several chunks of code from this book in your program or answering a question by citing our book and quoting example code does not require permission. But if you do choose to give credit, an attribution typically includes the title, author, publisher, and ISBN. For example, "PostgreSQL 16 Cookbook, Second Edition by Peter G".

If you are unsure whether your intended use of the code examples falls under fair use or the permissions outlined above, please do not hesitate to reach out to us at support@gitforgits.com.

We are happy to assist and clarify any concerns.

Acknowledgement

I owe a tremendous debt of gratitude to GitforGits, for their unflagging enthusiasm and wise counsel throughout the entire process of writing this book. Their knowledge and careful editing helped make sure the piece was useful for people of all reading levels and comprehension skills. In addition, I'd like to thank everyone involved in the publishing process for their efforts in making this book a reality. Their efforts, from copyediting to advertising, made the project what it is today.

Finally, I'd like to express my gratitude to everyone who has shown me unconditional love and encouragement throughout my life. Their support was crucial to the completion of this book. I appreciate your help with this endeavour and your continued interest in my career.

CHAPTER 1: PREPARING POSTGRESQL 16

Introduction

In this chapter, you will be exploring the foundational aspects of PostgreSQL 16.1, laying the groundwork for effective database management and optimization. You will be learning about the architecture of PostgreSQL, gaining insights into how its client-server model operates, and understanding the critical components that ensure efficient data processing. By delving into the auxiliary processes like the Background Writer, Checkpoint Process, and Write-Ahead Log (WAL) Writer, you will be discovering how PostgreSQL maintains data integrity and performance, providing a robust environment for applications.

You will also be focusing on the installation methods available for PostgreSQL, exploring both binary and source code approaches. You will be receiving step-by-step guidance on setting up PostgreSQL from binaries, ensuring a quick and straightforward installation, and you will also be exploring the benefits and processes of compiling PostgreSQL from source code. This will enable you to customize your setup to meet specific requirements, granting you greater control over your database environment. You will be learning how to configure post-installation settings to optimize your database for performance and reliability.

Furthermore, you will be understanding how to parse and interpret PostgreSQL startup logs, which will be crucial for diagnosing issues and maintaining smooth database operations. You will be gaining practical skills in analyzing log entries, identifying warnings and errors, and using logs to troubleshoot problems effectively. Additionally, you will be exploring the structural objects within PostgreSQL databases, including tables, indexes, sequences, views, and stored procedures, allowing you to design and manage efficient data architectures. And lastly, you will be diving into key configuration parameters that impact PostgreSQL's performance and functionality. You will be learning how to adjust settings like **`shared_buffers`**, **`work_mem`**, and **`max_connections`** to optimize your server's efficiency.

Recipe #1: Simplify PostgreSQL Architecture

PostgreSQL is a sophisticated open-source object-relational database management system (ORDBMS) renowned for its robustness, extensibility, and standards compliance. Understanding its architecture optimizes performance, troubleshoot issues, and leverage its full capabilities.

Core Components

Client-Server Model

- PostgreSQL operates on a client-server model where the server handles requests from clients. The server is the backbone of PostgreSQL operations, responsible for processing and managing client requests.

- The server runs as a background process (daemon) and listens for incoming connections. It manages database operations, transaction handling, and data integrity.
- Users and applications connect to the server through various interfaces, such as:
- Tools like **`psql`** allow direct interaction with the server, executing SQL commands and scripts.
- Applications like pgAdmin and DBeaver provide a visual interface for managing databases, building queries, and monitoring performance.
- Libraries such as libpq for C/C++ and JDBC for Java enable programmatic interaction with PostgreSQL.

Auxiliary Processes

PostgreSQL's architecture includes several background processes that enhance performance and maintain data consistency:

Background Writer

- Responsible for periodically writing dirty pages (modified data in memory) to disk, reducing the workload on the server during peak times.
- Ensures that the buffer pool remains available for new data, maintaining smooth operations.

Checkpoint Process

- Ensures data durability by forcing all modified pages to disk at regular intervals, creating a stable state on disk.
- Reduces recovery time in case of a crash by ensuring that the database can be quickly restored to its last consistent state.

Autovacuum Process

- Automatically reclaims storage by removing dead tuples left behind after updates and deletes, preventing table bloat.
- Maintains query performance by keeping tables clean and efficient.

Write-Ahead Log (WAL) Writer

- Logs all changes before they are applied to the database, providing a reliable recovery mechanism in case of failure.
- Supports transactional integrity and crash recovery by ensuring that committed transactions are never lost.

Data Storage Objects

PostgreSQL databases are organized into schemas, which contain various objects, including:

Tables

- Store data in rows and columns, forming the core of database storage.
- Support complex data types and constraints, enabling structured data storage and retrieval.

Indexes

- Enhance query performance by providing fast lookup capabilities for specific columns.
- Use various indexing methods, such as B-tree, hash, and GiST, to optimize access patterns.

Sequences

- Generate unique numeric values, often used for primary keys.
- Ensure that identifiers are consistently unique across tables.

Views

- Offer a virtual table representing the result of a stored query, providing simplified access to complex data.
- Enhance security by restricting direct access to underlying tables.

Stored Procedures

- Encapsulate business logic in the database, enabling complex operations on data.
- Support PL/pgSQL and other procedural languages for advanced scripting.

Query Execution Process

PostgreSQL processes queries through a series of steps, ensuring efficient and reliable data operations:

Parsing

- The server parses incoming SQL queries to check for syntax errors and generate a parse tree.
- Syntax validation ensures that only valid queries proceed to the next stage.

Planning

- The query planner and optimizer create an execution plan, selecting the most efficient way to execute the query.

- The planner considers factors such as data distribution, available indexes, and join strategies.

Execution

- The executor carries out the execution plan, retrieving or modifying data as specified by the query.
- Supports transaction management, ensuring that operations are atomic, consistent, isolated, and durable (ACID).

Result Return

- The server returns the result to the client, completing the query execution process.
- Supports various output formats, including plain text, JSON, and XML.

Practical Tips

To maximize performance and guarantee dependable data management, familiarity with PostgreSQL's architecture is necessary. Following are some practical tips:

- Proper indexing can significantly improve query performance. Analyze query patterns and create indexes to support common operations.
- Use tools like **`pg_stat_activity`** and **`pg_stat_bgwriter`** to monitor server activity and identify bottlenecks.
- Adjust settings in **`postgresql.conf`** to match your workload and hardware capabilities. Key parameters include **`shared_buffers`**, **`work_mem`**, and **`effective_cache_size`**.
- Schedule regular maintenance tasks, such as vacuuming and analyzing, to keep the database optimized and responsive.

If you want to create database solutions that can handle the demands of modern applications, you need to learn PostgreSQL's architecture. It's scalable, efficient, and robust.

Recipe #2: Installing PostgreSQL 16.1 from Binaries

Installing PostgreSQL from binaries is a quick and straightforward method to get your database server up and running. This approach is ideal for users who prefer a hassle-free setup without the need for compiling from source.

Step-by-step Installation

Ensure your system is up-to-date with the latest packages:

```
sudo apt-get update

sudo apt-get upgrade
```

Navigate to the PostgreSQL official download page and select Ubuntu. Then, choose the appropriate version (16.1) and download the binary package.

Then, import the GPG key for the repository:

```
wget --quiet -O -
https://www.postgresql.org/media/keys/ACCC4CF8.asc | sudo
apt-key add -
```

After this, add the PostgreSQL APT repository:

```
sudo sh -c 'echo "deb
http://apt.postgresql.org/pub/repos/apt/ $(lsb_release -
cs)-pgdg main" > /etc/apt/sources.list.d/pgdg.list'
```

Refresh the package list to include the new repository:

```
sudo apt-get update
```

Install PostgreSQL along with additional utilities:

```
sudo apt-get install postgresql-16 postgresql-contrib
```

Now verify the status using:

```
sudo systemctl status postgresql
```

Then, ensure PostgreSQL is running and configured to start on boot:

```
sudo systemctl start postgresql
```

```
sudo systemctl enable postgresql
```

Followed by, switch to the **postgres** user and start the **psql** shell:

```
sudo -i -u postgres

psql
```

Finally, you can now execute SQL commands to manage your databases.

Post-Installation Configuration

First, edit the **pg_hba.conf** file to configure client authentication:

```
sudo nano /etc/postgresql/16/main/pg_hba.conf
```

Then, add or modify entries to allow remote access as needed. For example:

```
host     all               all               192.168.1.0/24
md5
```

Edit the configuration file to set your preferred settings, such as memory usage, logging, and connection settings:

```
sudo nano /etc/postgresql/16/main/postgresql.conf
```

While doing so, important parameters to consider:

- **listen_addresses = '*'**: Allows connections from any IP address.
- **shared_buffers = 1GB**: Sets the amount of memory allocated for caching data.
- **max_connections = 100**: Limits the number of concurrent connections.

And then finally, apply the configuration changes by restarting the service:

```
sudo systemctl restart postgresql
```

Verification and Testing

To begin with the verification and testing, use **psql** to create a new database and verify the installation:

```
CREATE DATABASE testdb;

\c testdb

CREATE TABLE test_table (id SERIAL PRIMARY KEY, name
VARCHAR(50));

INSERT INTO test_table (name) VALUES ('PostgreSQL');

SELECT * FROM test_table;
```

Then, review PostgreSQL logs for any issues during startup or operation:

```
sudo tail -f /var/log/postgresql/postgresql-16-main.log
```

This step-by-step demonstration provides a curated approach to installing PostgreSQL 16.1 on a Linux system using binaries, ensuring that you have a working database server with all necessary components configured.

Recipe #3: Installing PostgreSQL 16.1 from Source Code

Installing PostgreSQL from source gives you full control over the installation process, allowing for custom configurations and optimizations tailored to specific requirements. This approach is beneficial for users who need a customized setup or are using an operating system not directly supported by binary packages.

Step-by-step Installation

To begin with, first visit the PostgreSQL source code page and download the tarball for version 16.1. And then, extract the tarball to a preferred directory:

```
tar -xvzf postgresql-16.1.tar.gz
```

```
cd postgresql-16.1
```

Then, do not forget to verify that the system has all necessary build tools and libraries:

```
sudo apt-get install build-essential libreadline-dev
zlib1g-dev flex bison
```

Next, run the configuration script to set up the build environment:

```
./configure --prefix=/usr/local/pgsql --with-openssl
```

Here, the **`--prefix`** option specifies the installation directory, and **`--with-openssl`** enables SSL support for secure connections.

Compile PostgreSQL

Now, compile the source code using the **`make`** command:

```
make
```

Install the compiled binaries and libraries:

```
sudo make install
```

Create a dedicated system user for running PostgreSQL:

```
sudo adduser postgres
```

Initialize the database cluster:

```
sudo mkdir /usr/local/pgsql/data

sudo chown postgres /usr/local/pgsql/data

sudo -u postgres /usr/local/pgsql/bin/initdb -D
/usr/local/pgsql/data
```

Set the environment variables for the PostgreSQL user:

```
echo "export PATH=$PATH:/usr/local/pgsql/bin" >>
~/.bashrc

source ~/.bashrc
```

Then, launch the PostgreSQL server process:

```
sudo -u postgres /usr/local/pgsql/bin/pg_ctl -D
/usr/local/pgsql/data -l logfile start
```

Now, connect to the server using **psql**:

```
sudo -u postgres /usr/local/pgsql/bin/psql
```

Post-Installation Configuration

For this, first set a password for the **postgres** user:

```
\password postgres
```

Then, modify **pg_hba.conf** to allow remote connections with appropriate authentication methods:

```
sudo nano /usr/local/pgsql/data/pg_hba.conf
```

Following is the example configuration:

```
host    all             all             0.0.0.0/0
md5
```

Edit **postgresql.conf** to allow connections from any IP:

```
sudo nano /usr/local/pgsql/data/postgresql.conf
```

In the above, set the **listen_addresses** parameter:

```
listen_addresses = '*'
```

And then, apply the configuration changes:

```
sudo -u postgres /usr/local/pgsql/bin/pg_ctl -D
/usr/local/pgsql/data restart
```

Verification and Testing

For this, create a sample database and perform basic operations to verify functionality:

```
CREATE DATABASE mydb;

\c mydb

CREATE TABLE test (id SERIAL PRIMARY KEY, data
VARCHAR(100));

INSERT INTO test (data) VALUES ('Hello, PostgreSQL!');

SELECT * FROM test;
```

Review the logfile for any errors or warnings during the startup process:

```
cat logfile
```

These steps successfully install the PostgreSQL 16.1 from source, thereby customizing the setup and also ensures a reliable and efficient database environment.

Recipe #4: Parsing Database Startup Logs

Understanding and analyzing PostgreSQL startup logs is essential for database administrators to diagnose issues, monitor server performance, and ensure smooth operations. The logs provide insights into the server configuration, startup processes, and potential errors that can impact database functionality.

The PostgreSQL logs are a valuable resource for:

- To help track server activity and performance metrics, allowing administrators to identify and address bottlenecks.
- To provide detailed information about errors and warnings, facilitating troubleshooting and problem resolution.
- Provide audit database access and activities, enhancing security and compliance efforts.

Parsing PostgreSQL Logs

By default, PostgreSQL logs are stored in the **pg_log** directory within the data directory. The location can be adjusted in the **postgresql.conf** file under the **log_directory** parameter.

To identify the log directory, check the configuration:

```
sudo nano /etc/postgresql/16/main/postgresql.conf
```

Look for the following parameters:

```
log_directory = 'pg_log'

log_filename = 'postgresql-%Y-%m-%d_%H%M%S.log'
```

Open the most recent log file. For example, using **nano**:

```
nano /path/to/pg_log/postgresql-2024-08-05_000000.log
```

These log entries are timestamped and include details about events during startup and operation:

```
2024-08-05 12:34:56.789 EDT [12345] LOG:  database system
is ready to accept connections
```

In the above example, try focussing on the following key components:

- **Timestamps**: Indicate when events occurred, helping track the sequence of operations.
- **Process IDs**: Identify the process responsible for the event, useful for correlating related entries.
- **Log Levels**: Indicate the severity of the event, such as **LOG**, **WARNING**, **ERROR**, or **FATAL**.

Next, search for lines indicating warnings or errors, as these are crucial for troubleshooting:

```
2024-08-05 12:35:01.234 EDT [12345] ERROR:  relation
"missing_table" does not exist
```

Here, try to look for common issues:

- Misconfigured parameters in `postgresql.conf` or `pg_hba.conf`.
- Issues with client authentication or network connectivity.
- Corrupted data or missing relations.

These settings provide more context about the events, including the user, database, and query responsible for the action.

Sample Program: Troubleshooting a Startup Error

Consider a scenario where the PostgreSQL server fails to start due to a configuration error. To fix it, first open the most recent log file and search for the **FATAL** error message:

```
2024-08-05 12:40:00.456 EDT [12345] FATAL:  could not
access private key file "server.key": Permission denied
```

Here, the error indicates that PostgreSQL cannot access the private key file required for SSL connections. This is often due to incorrect file permissions.

To fix it, adjust the permissions of the key file to ensure that the PostgreSQL process can access it:

```
sudo chown postgres:postgres /etc/ssl/private/server.key

sudo chmod 600 /etc/ssl/private/server.key
```

After resolving the permission issue, restart the PostgreSQL service and verify that it starts successfully:

Recipe #5: Discovering PostgreSQL Database Structural Objects

PostgreSQL databases consist of various structural objects, each serving specific roles in data management. Understanding these objects and their relationships is key to effective database administration and application development.

Key Structural Objects

Tables

- Tables are the fundamental units of data storage in PostgreSQL, organizing data into rows and columns.
- It stores structured data, enforce constraints (e.g., primary keys, foreign keys), and support various data types.

For example:

```
CREATE TABLE employees (

  employee_id SERIAL PRIMARY KEY,

  first_name VARCHAR(50),

  last_name VARCHAR(50),

  email VARCHAR(100) UNIQUE,

  hire_date DATE

);
```

Indexes

- It indexes improve data retrieval speed by providing fast lookup capabilities for specific columns.
- It enhances query performance, especially for large tables with frequent read operations.

For example:

```
CREATE INDEX idx_employees_email ON employees(email);
```

Sequences

- The sequences generate unique numeric values, often used for primary keys.

- It ensures that identifiers are consistently unique across tables, supporting auto-increment functionality.

For example:

```
CREATE SEQUENCE employee_id_seq START WITH 1 INCREMENT BY
1;
```

Views

- Views offer a virtual table representing the result of a stored query, providing simplified access to complex data.
- It simplifies the query logic, enhance security by restricting direct access to underlying tables, and provide a consistent interface for applications.

For example:

```
CREATE VIEW active_employees AS

SELECT employee_id, first_name, last_name

FROM employees

WHERE active = TRUE;
```

Stored Procedures

- Stored procedures encapsulate business logic and enable complex operations on data.
- It automates repetitive tasks, enforce business rules, and support procedural logic with languages like PL/pgSQL.

For example:

```
CREATE PROCEDURE update_salary(emp_id INT, new_salary
NUMERIC)

LANGUAGE plpgsql

AS $$

BEGIN
```

```
  UPDATE employees SET salary = new_salary WHERE
employee_id = emp_id;

END;

$$;
```

Discovering Structural Objects

To do this, use an access solution to connect to your database. For example, using **psql**:

```
psql -U postgres -d mydatabase
```

Display all databases on the server:

```
\l
```

Switch to the desired database:

```
\c mydatabase
```

View all schemas within the selected database:

```
\dn
```

List the tables, indexes, sequences, views, and functions in the selected schema:

```
\dt

\di

\ds

\dv

\df
```

You can also use additional commands to explore the properties and relationships of database objects.

Sample Program: Analyzing Database Structure

Consider a scenario where you need to analyze the structure of a database used for an employee management system:

List All Tables

Display the tables in the public schema:

```
\dt public.*
```

Describe a Specific Table

View detailed information about the **employees** table:

```
\d employees
```

The output will include columns, data types, constraints, and indexes.

Identify Indexes

List indexes associated with the **employees** table:

```
\di+ employees*
```

Analyze Views

Display views that provide a summary of active employees:

```
\dv+ active_employees
```

Explore Stored Procedures

List stored procedures related to employee management:

```
\df+ update_salary
```

By utilizing these objects, you can optimize data storage, retrieval, and manipulation, ensuring that your applications run smoothly and efficiently.

Recipe #6: Understanding Use of Key Configuration Parameters

PostgreSQL also provides numerous configuration parameters that can be adjusted to optimize performance, enhance functionality, and tailor the server to specific workload requirements. Knowing and fine-tuning these parameters maximizes server efficiency.

Key Configuration Parameters

shared_buffers

- It determines the amount of memory allocated for caching data in shared memory buffers.
- By increasing this value can improve read performance by reducing the frequency of disk reads.
- It is recommended to be set at 25-40% of system RAM.

Following is the sample configuration:

```
shared_buffers = 4GB
```

work_mem

- This one specifies the amount of memory allocated for sorting and hashing operations.
- The higher values can improve query performance, especially for complex operations involving sorting and aggregation.
- It is recommended to adjust based on workload requirements and available memory.

Following is the sample configuration:

```
work_mem = 16MB
```

maintenance_work_mem

- It allocates memory for maintenance tasks like vacuuming and indexing.
- By increasing this value can speed up maintenance processes, reducing downtime.
- It is generally set higher for large databases with frequent maintenance needs.

Following is the sample configuration:

```
maintenance_work_mem = 512MB
```

effective_cache_size

- This one estimates the size of the operating system's disk cache, guiding the query planner's decisions.
- It helps the planner make informed decisions about query execution plans, improving performance.
- It is set to approximately 75% of system RAM.

Following is the sample configuration:

```
effective_cache_size = 12GB
```

max_connections

- This one limits the number of concurrent connections to the server.
- The balance of this value is important for resource management, preventing excessive load on the server.
- It is set based on expected user load and application requirements.

Following is the sample configuration:

```
max_connections = 200
```

checkpoint_timeout

- This one specifies the frequency at which checkpoints are performed.
- Its longer intervals reduce I/O overhead but increase recovery time after a crash.
- The balance is based on transaction volume and recovery requirements.

Following is the sample configuration:

```
checkpoint_timeout = 15min
```

autovacuum

- It controls the automatic vacuuming of tables and indexes to prevent bloat.

- By enabling this parameter, it helps maintain database performance by cleaning up dead rows.

Following is the sample configuration:

```
autovacuum = on
```

wal_buffers

- This one sets the amount of memory allocated for Write-Ahead Logging (WAL) buffers.
- The larger buffers can improve transaction throughput, especially in write-heavy environments.
- It is generally set higher for systems with high transaction volumes.

Following is the sample configuration:

```
wal_buffers = 16MB
```

Understanding and configuring PostgreSQL's key parameters helps optimizing server performance and ensuring that your database can handle demanding workloads efficiently. By tailoring settings, you can achieve a balance between performance, reliability, and resource utilization.

Summary

This chapter taught about the essential components and functionalities of PostgreSQL 16.1. You gained an in-depth understanding of PostgreSQL's architecture, including its client-server model and auxiliary processes such as the Background Writer, Checkpoint Process, and Write-Ahead Log (WAL) Writer. These insights allowed you to appreciate how PostgreSQL maintains data integrity and ensures efficient data processing in various applications. The chapter also covered different installation methods, providing step-by-step instructions for installing PostgreSQL from binaries and source code. This equipped you with the knowledge to set up PostgreSQL environments tailored to your specific needs and requirements.

The chapter also focused on interpreting PostgreSQL startup logs, a vital skill for diagnosing issues and ensuring smooth database operations. You learned how to parse log entries, identify warnings and errors, and use logs for troubleshooting. Additionally, you explored PostgreSQL's structural objects, such as tables, indexes, sequences, views, and stored procedures, allowing you to understand how these elements form the foundation of efficient database design and management.

Furthermore, you delved into key configuration parameters that influence PostgreSQL's performance and functionality. You learned how to adjust settings like **shared_buffers**, **work_mem**, and **max_connections** to optimize server efficiency and meet the demands of their applications. By the end of the chapter, you had acquired a solid foundation in managing and configuring PostgreSQL databases, equipping you with the skills necessary to ensure reliability, scalability, and speed in your database environments.

Chapter 2: Performing Basic PostgreSQL Operations

Introduction

In this chapter, you will be delving into fundamental PostgreSQL operations using the AdventureWorks database as a practical tool. You will be learning about creating schemas and organizing data within a PostgreSQL environment, focusing on how schemas can enhance data management, security, and collaboration. You will also be exploring various indexing techniques available and their application to optimize query performance. You will be learning how to choose the right indexing strategy based on data types and query patterns, gaining insights into how indexes can significantly improve data retrieval times. Through practical examples, you will be understanding how to apply different indexing methods, such as B-tree, Hash, GiST, SP-GiST, GIN, and BRIN, to enhance the performance of the AdventureWorks database.

Additionally, you will be focusing on advanced query techniques using Common Table Expressions (CTEs) and recursive queries. You will be discovering how to simplify complex queries using the **WITH** clause, breaking them down into logical components that improve readability and maintainability. By the end of this chapter, you will have gained a detailed understanding of basic PostgreSQL operations, equipping you with the skills to manage and optimize databases using schemas, indexing, and advanced query techniques.

Recipe #1: Exploring AdventureWorks Database

In this chapter, we utilized the **AdventureWorks** database as a simple educational tool, designed to simulate real-world business scenarios for database professionals and application developers. This sample database represents a fictional company, Adventure Works Cycles, a manufacturer of bicycles and accessories, providing an extensive range of tables, views, stored procedures, and other database objects. The database is available in the following URL:

https://github.com/kittenpub/database-repository/blob/main/data.zip

This database is organized into several schemas, each representing different business domains within the company:

Production Schema

- This manages manufacturing and production processes.
- It includes tables for products, product categories, product models, work orders, and bill of materials. It also contains data about product descriptions, manufacturing steps, and product inventory.

Following is the sample table: **production.products**

```
SELECT product_id, product_name, product_number
```

```
FROM production.products;
```

Sales Schema

- This schema tracks sales-related information.
- It manages customers, sales orders, sales order details, sales territories, and salespersons. It also covers shipping, billing addresses, and special offers.

Following is the example table: **sales.orders**

```
SELECT order_id, order_date, customer_id, total_due

FROM sales.orders;
```

Purchasing Schema

- This particular schema handles the procurement process for raw materials.
- It consists of data about vendors, purchase orders, purchase order details, and vendor contacts.

Following is the example table: **purchasing.vendors**

```
SELECT vendor_id, vendor_name, contact_name

FROM purchasing.vendors;
```

HumanResources Schema

- This one manages employee-related data.
- It includes tables for employee information, job titles, pay structures, and departmental hierarchies. It also handles employee shifts and attendance.

Following is the example table: **humanresources.employees**

```
SELECT employee_id, first_name, last_name, job_title

FROM humanresources.employees;
```

Person Schema

- It cntralizes data about people involved with the company.
- This schema stores personal details of employees, customers, vendors, and contacts, including names, addresses, email addresses, and phone numbers.

Following is the example table: **person.contacts**

```
SELECT contact_id, first_name, last_name, email_address

FROM person.contacts;
```

dbo Schema

- It houses miscellaneous database objects that do not belong to a specific business area.
- Contains general-purpose tables and objects used across different domains.

Following is the example table: **dbo.misc_data**

```
SELECT data_id, data_value

FROM dbo.misc_data;
```

This AdventureWorks database serves as an ideal resource for practicing various database tasks, providing a realistic environment that reflects the complexities and intricacies of real-world business processes. This understanding prepares you for more advanced topics in PostgreSQL.

Recipe #2: Selecting Right Database Schema

PostgreSQL's schema system is a powerful feature that allows you to organize database objects into logical groups, improving manageability, security, and performance. In this recipe, we explored the concept of defining PostgreSQL schemas, their types, and how to create and manage them effectively.

Understanding PostgreSQL Schema Types

Public Schema

This is the default schema created in every new PostgreSQL database. It is accessible to all users with database access. It is suitable for general-purpose objects that need to be widely accessible.

Private Schema

This one is created by a user, accessible only to the owner or those granted explicit permissions. It is ideal for organizing objects that require restricted access, enhancing security.

Creating Schemas

Creating a new schema is straightforward. The **CREATE SCHEMA** command is used to define a schema within the current database:

```
CREATE SCHEMA sales;
```

This command creates a schema named "sales." By default, it is created in the current database's search path. You can also specify the owner of the schema:

```
CREATE SCHEMA sales AUTHORIZATION sales_user;
```

In this example, the schema "sales" is owned by the user "sales_user," allowing them to manage objects within the schema.

Moving Objects Between Schemas

You can move database objects between schemas using the **ALTER** command. For example, to move a table from one schema to another:

```
ALTER TABLE sales.orders SET SCHEMA archive;
```

This command moves the "orders" table from the "sales" schema to the "archive" schema.

Benefits of using Schemas

- Schemas organize database objects into logical groups, simplifying management and maintenance.
- Private schemas restrict access to objects, protecting sensitive data.
- Schemas provide a clear organizational structure, aiding team collaboration and development.
- Organizing objects into schemas can optimize query performance by reducing the number of queries needed to retrieve data.

Databases in PostgreSQL can be better organized with the help of schemas, which group objects logically and make them easy to find. This method not only makes management easier but also boosts security and performance.

Recipe #3: Selecting Indexing Techniques

Indexing significantly impacts the query performance and overall efficiency. PostgreSQL offers a variety of indexing techniques, each designed to handle specific data types and query patterns. In this recipe, we explored the different indexing techniques supported by PostgreSQL and how they can be applied to optimize the AdventureWorks database.

Indexing Techniques in PostgreSQL

B-tree Indexing

This is a default indexing technique in PostgreSQL, optimized for data that can be sorted, such as numbers or text. It is primarily suitable for range queries and general-purpose indexing.

For example:

```
CREATE INDEX idx_order_id ON sales.orders(order_id);
```

Hash Indexing

This is an indexing method that uses hash functions, optimized for equality comparisons. It is considered ideal for queries that involve exact matches on indexed columns.

For example:

```
CREATE INDEX idx_customer_id ON sales.customers USING
HASH (customer_id);
```

GiST Indexing (Generalized Search Tree)

This one supports complex data types and custom search algorithms. It is very useful for geometric shapes, text search, and other complex data types.

For example:

```
CREATE INDEX idx_product_geom ON production.products
USING GiST (geom);
```

SP-GiST Indexing (Space-Partitioned Generalized Search Tree)

This one is primarily optimized for spatial data and other partitioned datasets. And it is found to be very effective for spatial indexing and hierarchical data.

For example:

```
CREATE INDEX idx_product_geom ON production.products
USING SPGIST (geom);
```

GIN Indexing (Generalized Inverted Index)

This particular indexing is designed for indexing array data types and full-text search and found be suitable for full-text search and multi-valued fields.

For example:

```
CREATE INDEX idx_product_tags ON production.products
USING GIN (tags);
```

BRIN Indexing (Block Range INdex)

This proves to be very efficient for large tables with sequentially ordered data, and considered to be ideal for data with block-level correlations, such as time-series data.

For example:

```
CREATE INDEX idx_orders_date ON sales.orders USING BRIN
(order_date);
```

Optimizing Database

Consider our AdventureWorks database, which has a large table containing sales data. You might need to optimize queries for specific scenarios:

Optimize Sales Orders by Date

Use a BRIN index on the **order_date** column to speed up queries that filter by date ranges:

```
CREATE INDEX idx_orders_date ON sales.orders USING BRIN
(order_date);
```

Improve Full-Text Search on Product Descriptions

Use a GIN index on the **description** column to enhance full-text search capabilities:

```
CREATE INDEX idx_product_descriptions ON
production.product_descriptions USING GIN
(to_tsvector('english', description));
```

Enhance Query Performance for Customer Lookups

Use a B-tree index on the **customer_id** column for frequent queries based on customer identifiers:

```
CREATE INDEX idx_customer_id ON sales.customers
(customer_id);
```

By understanding the different types of indexes and their use cases, you can select the most appropriate indexing strategy for your data and queries, ensuring efficient and effective database operations. By leveraging indexing techniques in the AdventureWorks database, you can practice optimizing queries and understanding the impact of different indexing strategies on performance.

Recipe #4: Preparing Database Log Directory

The log directory stores log files that contain information about database activities and errors. These logs are invaluable for monitoring database activity, troubleshooting errors, and optimizing performance. In this recipe, we prepared the log directory for the database, enabling administrators to effectively manage and analyze logs.

Setting up the Log Directory

Use the following command to create a directory for PostgreSQL logs:

```
sudo mkdir /var/log/postgresql
```

This command creates a directory named **postgresql** in the **/var/log** directory. Then, assign the directory ownership to the PostgreSQL user to ensure proper permissions:

```
sudo chown postgres:postgres /var/log/postgresql
```

This command changes the ownership to the **postgres** user, allowing PostgreSQL to write logs to this directory.

Open the PostgreSQL configuration file using a text editor:

```
sudo nano /etc/postgresql/16/main/postgresql.conf
```

Locate and modify the following parameters to enable logging and specify the log directory:

```
logging_collector = on

log_directory = '/var/log/postgresql'

log_filename = 'postgresql-%Y-%m-%d_%H%M%S.log'

log_truncate_on_rotation = on

log_rotation_age = 1d

log_rotation_size = 10MB
```

Using 'logging_collector'

The **logging_collector** parameter must be set to **on** to activate log collection. This enables the logging collector process, which captures log messages and writes them to files. Then, apply the configuration changes:

```
sudo systemctl restart postgresql
```

The **log_filename** parameter defines the log file naming convention, while **log_rotation_age** and **log_rotation_size** manage log rotation based on age and size. And, keep adjusting these parameters to suit your needs. Overall, setting up a dedicated log directory and enabling detailed logging, one can ensure that the database is well-monitored and that issues can be diagnosed and resolved efficiently.

Recipe #5: Using PostgreSQL TOAST

PostgreSQL's TOAST (The Oversized-Attribute Storage Technique) is a mechanism designed to handle large data types like **text**, **xml**, and **bytea**. It efficiently stores large data attributes in a separate table, saving disk space and improving database performance. In this recipe, we explored how to utilize TOAST within the database.

Using TOAST

To begin with, first define a table with a large data type column:

```
CREATE TABLE production.product_descriptions (
  product_id INT PRIMARY KEY,
  description TEXT
);
```

Here, the **description** column uses the **TEXT** data type, which is managed by TOAST when the data size exceeds the threshold.

Then, insert records into the **product_descriptions** table:

```
INSERT INTO production.product_descriptions VALUES
(1, 'Lorem ipsum dolor sit amet, consectetur adipiscing elit.'),
(2, 'Nulla facilisi. Vestibulum eleifend augue ut turpis suscipit at varius enim sagittis.'),
(3, 'Phasellus consectetur dolor sit amet efficitur porttitor nunc lacus sollicitudin orci vel lobortis arcu justo vel nibh.'),
(4, 'Donec gravida felis quis enim dapibus vel eleifend turpis tempor.'),
(5, 'Nam porttitor elementum risus id iaculis enim semper ut.');
```

Viewing TOASTed Data

PostgreSQL automatically manages TOAST data, and users typically don't interact directly with TOAST tables. However, you can query the **pg_toast** namespace to inspect TOAST tables:

```
SELECT relname FROM pg_class WHERE relname LIKE
'pg_toast_%';
```

TOAST minimizes the performance impact of storing large data by splitting it into manageable chunks. This improves access times for large objects. By storing large attributes in separate tables, TOAST reduces the space required for main tables, optimizing disk usage. The use of TOAST is an effective way to manage large data types without compromising performance.

Recipe #6: Creating and Administering PostgreSQL Temporary Tables

Temporary tables are used to store transient data that is only needed for the duration of a database session or transaction. They are valuable for managing intermediate results, performing complex calculations, and simplifying query logic. In this recipe, we explored how to create and use temporary tables in the database.

Creating Temporary Tables

Use the **CREATE TEMP TABLE** command to define a temporary table:

```
CREATE TEMP TABLE sales.temp_orders AS

SELECT * FROM sales.orders WHERE order_date = '2023-03-
22';
```

This above command creates a temporary table named **temp_orders** in the **sales** schema, populated with orders from March 22, 2023. These temporary tables can be used like regular tables but are session-specific. They allow complex operations without affecting permanent tables:

```
SELECT * FROM sales.temp_orders WHERE total_due > 1000;
```

Temporary tables are also automatically dropped at the end of the session or transaction. However, you can manually drop them if needed:

```
DROP TABLE IF EXISTS sales.temp_orders;
```

Sample Program: Performing Data Analysis

Consider a scenario where you need to analyze sales data for a specific day without altering the main orders table:

- Extract daily sales data into a temporary table:

```
CREATE TEMP TABLE daily_sales AS

SELECT product_id, SUM(quantity) AS total_quantity,
SUM(total_due) AS total_revenue

FROM sales.order_details

WHERE order_date = CURRENT_DATE

GROUP BY product_id;
```

- Perform analysis on the temporary data without impacting the main database:

```
SELECT product_id, total_quantity, total_revenue

FROM daily_sales

WHERE total_revenue > 5000;
```

- Use temporary tables for session-specific calculations, ensuring that data remains isolated and operations do not interfere with other sessions.

To sum up, temporary tables are a powerful tool for managing transient data and performing complex calculations in PostgreSQL. Leveraging temporary tables enhances their data analysis capabilities and streamline query logic, making them an essential resource for database administrators and developers.

Recipe #7: Using SELECT in WITH Queries

The **WITH** clause, also known as Common Table Expressions (CTE), is used to define temporary result sets that can be referenced within a **SELECT**, **INSERT**, **UPDATE**, or **DELETE** statement. CTEs are particularly useful for breaking down complex queries into simpler, more manageable parts. In this recipe, we explored how to use the **SELECT** statement within **WITH** queries using the database.

Understanding CTEs

A CTE is a named temporary result set defined within a **WITH** clause, which precedes the main query. CTEs enhance query readability and can be reused multiple times within a query, providing a more structured approach to writing SQL queries.

We will create a simple CTE to calculate total sales for a specific date:

```
WITH sales_today AS (

  SELECT order_id, customer_id, total_due

  FROM sales.orders

  WHERE order_date = '2023-03-22'

)

SELECT COUNT(order_id) AS total_orders, SUM(total_due) AS
total_sales

FROM sales_today;
```

In the above program, the **sales_today** CTE retrieves orders placed on March 22, 2023. The main query then calculates the total number of orders and sales.

Using Multiple CTEs

Now, CTEs can be chained together to create more complex queries as shown below:

```
WITH sales_today AS (

  SELECT order_id, customer_id, total_due

  FROM sales.orders

  WHERE order_date = '2023-03-22'

),
```

```
customer_totals AS (
  SELECT customer_id, SUM(total_due) AS customer_total
  FROM sales_today
  GROUP BY customer_id
)
SELECT c.customer_id, c.first_name, c.last_name,
ct.customer_total
FROM customer_totals ct
JOIN sales.customers c ON c.customer_id = ct.customer_id
ORDER BY ct.customer_total DESC;
```

Here, the first CTE **sales_today** selects orders from a specific day, while the second CTE **customer_totals** aggregates sales by customer. The main query retrieves customer details and their total sales, sorted by the highest sales first.

The purpose of CTE is to:

- Break down complex queries into logical steps, making them easier to understand and maintain.
- Get referenced multiple times within the same query, eliminating the need for duplicate code.
- Allow complex logic to be encapsulated in smaller, modular components, facilitating query optimization.

Sample Program: Analyzing Sales Performance

Consider a scenario where you need to analyze sales performance across different regions:

First, define CTEs for Regional Sales. For this, use CTEs to calculate total sales for each region:

```
WITH regional_sales AS (
  SELECT territory_id, SUM(total_due) AS territory_sales
```

```
  FROM sales.orders
  GROUP BY territory_id
),
territory_names AS (
  SELECT territory_id, territory_name
  FROM sales.territories
)
SELECT tn.territory_name, rs.territory_sales
FROM regional_sales rs
JOIN territory_names tn ON rs.territory_id =
tn.territory_id
ORDER BY rs.territory_sales DESC;
```

The first CTE **regional_sales** calculates total sales by territory, and the second CTE **territory_names** retrieves territory names. The main query joins these CTEs to display sales figures for each region.

To sum up, the use of **SELECT** in **WITH** queries is a powerful technique for simplifying complex SQL queries and improving their readability and maintainability.

Recipe #8: Running Recursive Queries

PostgreSQL supports recursive queries using the **WITH RECURSIVE** clause, which allows queries to reference their own output. Recursive queries are especially useful for querying hierarchical data structures, such as organizational charts or product categories. In this recipe, we explored how to run recursive queries using the database.

Understanding Recursive Queries

Recursive queries consist of two parts: a base query and a recursive query. The base query defines the starting point, while the recursive query repeatedly references the result set until the desired hierarchy or condition is met.

Following are the benefits of Recursive Queries:

- It efficiently navigates hierarchical data structures, extracting complex relationships with ease.
- They are ideal for analyzing data that naturally forms a tree structure, such as categories, bills of materials, or organizational hierarchies.
- It reduces the need for complex joins and loops, making SQL code cleaner and more maintainable.

For example, we will create a recursive query to traverse product categories:

```
WITH RECURSIVE category_hierarchy AS (

  SELECT category_id, category_name, parent_category_id

  FROM production.categories

  WHERE parent_category_id IS NULL

  UNION ALL

  SELECT c.category_id, c.category_name,
c.parent_category_id

  FROM production.categories c

  JOIN category_hierarchy ch ON ch.category_id =
c.parent_category_id

)

SELECT * FROM category_hierarchy;
```

In the above code snippet, the base query selects top-level categories (those with no parent), while the recursive query joins the result with the **categories** table to find subcategories. This continues until all levels of the hierarchy are retrieved.

Recursive Queries for Organizational Charts

These recursive queries can also be used to explore employee hierarchies:

```
WITH RECURSIVE employee_hierarchy AS (
  SELECT employee_id, first_name, last_name, manager_id
  FROM humanresources.employees
  WHERE manager_id IS NULL
  UNION ALL
  SELECT e.employee_id, e.first_name, e.last_name,
e.manager_id
  FROM humanresources.employees e
  JOIN employee_hierarchy eh ON eh.employee_id =
e.manager_id
)
SELECT * FROM employee_hierarchy;
```

This query starts with top-level employees (those without a manager) and recursively retrieves their subordinates, effectively mapping the entire organizational structure.

Sample Program: Exploring Product Categories

Consider a scenario where you need to list all product categories and their subcategories. Here, we use a recursive query to explore category relationships as shown below:

```
WITH RECURSIVE product_categories AS (
  SELECT category_id, category_name, parent_category_id
  FROM production.categories
  WHERE parent_category_id IS NULL
  UNION ALL
```

```
  SELECT c.category_id, c.category_name,
c.parent_category_id

  FROM production.categories c

  JOIN product_categories pc ON pc.category_id =
c.parent_category_id

)

SELECT category_name, parent_category_id

FROM product_categories

ORDER BY parent_category_id, category_id;
```

This query retrieves all categories, displaying them in hierarchical order, showing which categories are subcategories of others. By employing recursive queries in the database, users can perform complex data analysis and reporting tasks with clarity and efficiency, leveraging PostgreSQL's advanced capabilities.

Summary

To summarize, you learned essential PostgreSQL operations wherein you explored the importance of schemas for organizing and managing data, enhancing database security and collaboration. You understood how to create and utilize schemas effectively to improve database manageability. The chapter covered various indexing techniques, including B-tree, Hash, GiST, SP-GiST, GIN, and BRIN, which are crucial for optimizing query performance. You learned how to select appropriate indexing strategies based on data types and query patterns, allowing you to significantly improve data retrieval times and overall database efficiency.

Additionally, the chapter introduced advanced query techniques using Common Table Expressions (CTEs) and recursive queries. You discovered how to simplify complex queries using the WITH clause, breaking them into manageable parts to enhance readability and maintainability. You also explored the use of recursive queries to navigate hierarchical data structures, effectively managing scenarios like organizational charts and product categories within the database. In short, you re skilled to manage and optimize databases using schemas, indexing, and advanced query techniques.

CHAPTER 3: POSTGRESQL CLOUD PROVISIONING

Introduction

In this chapter, you will be learning how to create and manage a PostgreSQL instance with Amazon RDS, leveraging its features to handle database workloads efficiently. This will involve setting up a PostgreSQL cloud instance, connecting to it through AWS EC2, and importing the database for real-world application. You will be discovering how to perform backup and restore operations using native PostgreSQL tools on AWS, ensuring data integrity and availability. You will be learning to create backups using **`pg_dump`**, store them in Amazon S3 for long-term storage, and restore them when necessary.

Furthermore, you will be focusing on database replication strategies to enhance performance and ensure high availability. You will be exploring the use of AWS RDS read replicas to offload read traffic and improve scalability. Additionally, you will be understanding bi-directional replication using the **`pglogical`** extension, enabling changes to be synchronized across multiple PostgreSQL instances.

By the end of this chapter, you will have gained practical experience in deploying and managing PostgreSQL databases in the cloud, using AWS tools to enhance performance, security, and availability.

Recipe #1: Create PostgreSQL AWS Instance and Manage Database Connection

This recipe focused on setting up a PostgreSQL instance in the cloud using Amazon Web Services (AWS), specifically through Amazon RDS (Relational Database Service), and managing connections using an EC2 instance.

Configure RDS Instance

- Ensure you have an AWS account. Log into the AWS Management Console and select your preferred region.
- Navigate to RDS in the AWS Management Console, and initiate the database creation process.
- Choose "Standard Create" for more configuration options, then select PostgreSQL as the database engine.
- Opt for the desired version and select the "Free tier" template for testing or "Production" for a robust setup.
- Enter a unique DB instance identifier, a master username, and a password.

- Select an appropriate instance class based on your requirements. And, configure storage options such as type and autoscaling settings.

Connect to RDS Instance using pgAdmin

- Ensure the instance is publicly accessible if needed. Choose or create a security group that permits inbound traffic on port 5432. This security group configuration allows connectivity from specific IP addresses or ranges, which is vital for remote database access.
- Set the initial database name to "adventureworks" during setup. Modify security settings as needed to permit inbound traffic from your local machine or application servers.
- Download the AdventureWorks database from the provided link. Extract the contents locally. Update the inbound rules for the associated security group to allow access from your IP address, ensuring connectivity to the database.
- Install and open pgAdmin. Add a new server connection using the RDS endpoint and the credentials you configured earlier. Use the pgAdmin Query Tool to run the AdventureWorks SQL script and populate your database.

Launch and Connect EC2 Instance

- Create a new EC2 instance for additional connectivity and processing capabilities, ensuring it is in the same VPC as the RDS instance for seamless integration.
- Select an Amazon Machine Image (AMI) and instance type based on your needs, then configure storage, security groups, and SSH access.
- SSH into your EC2 instance and install PostgreSQL client tools:

```
sudo yum update -y

sudo yum install -y postgresql
```

- Connect to your RDS instance from the EC2 instance using **`psql`**:

```
psql --host=<RDS_ENDPOINT> --port=5432 --
username=<MASTER_USERNAME> --password --
dbname=adventureworks
```

This recipe allowed you to create a scalable and flexible cloud-based PostgreSQL database using AWS services, managing connections through both pgAdmin and an EC2 instance. By following these steps, you ensured that the database was correctly set up and accessible in AWS.

Recipe #2: Native Backup/Restore with AWS EC2 Instance

This recipe demonstrated how to perform native PostgreSQL backups and restores on an EC2 instance, using AWS S3 for long-term storage. The process ensures that your AdventureWorks database is safely backed up and can be restored as needed.

Backup the Database

- SSH into your EC2 instance using the appropriate credentials.
- Create a directory on your EC2 instance to store backups:

```
mkdir ~/adventureworks_backups
```

- Use **pg_dump** to create a backup of the database:

```
pg_dump --host=<RDS_ENDPOINT> --port=5432 --
username=<MASTER_USERNAME> --password --format=custom --
file=~/adventureworks_backups/adventureworks_backup.dump
--dbname=adventureworks
```

- Enter your master password when prompted to create a binary dump file.

Restore the Database from Backup

- Install the AWS CLI if not already installed:

```
sudo yum install -y awscli
```

- Configure the AWS CLI:

```
aws configure
```

- Create an S3 bucket for backup storage:

```
aws s3api create-bucket --bucket adventureworks-backups-
<YOUR_NAME> --region <YOUR_REGION> --create-bucket-
configuration LocationConstraint=<YOUR_REGION>
```

- Upload the backup file to S3:

```
aws s3 cp
~/adventureworks_backups/adventureworks_backup.dump
s3://adventureworks-backups-
<YOUR_NAME>/adventureworks_backup.dump
```

- Create a new database on your RDS instance for restoration:

```
CREATE DATABASE adventureworks_restore;
```

- Use **pg_restore** to restore the backup:

```
pg_restore --host=<RDS_ENDPOINT> --port=5432 --
username=<MASTER_USERNAME> --password --
dbname=adventureworks_restore --verbose
~/adventureworks_backups/adventureworks_backup.dump
```

- Connect to the restored database and verify its contents:

```
psql --host=<RDS_ENDPOINT> --port=5432 --
username=<MASTER_USERNAME> --password --
dbname=adventureworks_restore
```

- Use **\dt** to list tables and confirm data integrity by running queries.

By following these steps, you ensured your database was backed up securely and restored successfully, utilizing AWS EC2 and S3 services to manage backup storage and retrieval effectively.

Recipe #3: Natively Backup/Restore with AWS RDS Instance

This recipe explored the use of AWS RDS features to manage backups through automated and manual snapshots, demonstrating how to restore the AdventureWorks database from these snapshots.

Create Manual Snapshot

- Navigate to the RDS Dashboard, select your AdventureWorks RDS instance, and click "Modify."
- Set the backup retention period to a non-zero value, enabling automated backups.
- On the RDS Dashboard, select the RDS instance and choose "Take snapshot" from the "Actions" menu. And then, provide a unique name for the snapshot and start the creation process.

Restore from Snapshot and Verify Resoration

- Go to the "Snapshots" section in the RDS Dashboard and select the desired snapshot.
- Choose "Restore snapshot" from the "Actions" menu. Configure the new RDS instance settings, such as instance class, storage, and network configuration, then click "Restore DB Instance."
- Once the new instance is available, connect to it using pgAdmin or **`psql`**.

If switching to the restored database, update your application's database connection settings to point to the new RDS instance endpoint.

Recipe #4: Manage Connection to Database on AWS

In this recipe, you learned how to manage connections to your PostgreSQL database hosted on AWS, ensuring security and performance through proper configuration and monitoring.

Modify Security Group Rules

- Log into the AWS Management Console and navigate to the RDS Dashboard. Select the RDS instance hosting the database.
- Locate the "Security group rules" section and click on the associated security group.

- Go to the "Inbound rules" tab and click "Edit inbound rules."
- Add a new rule to allow PostgreSQL traffic:
    - **Type**: PostgreSQL
    - **Protocol**: TCP
    - **Port range**: 5432
    - **Source**: Choose "My IP" to allow access from your current IP, or specify a custom IP range for broader access.
- Click "Save rules" to apply the changes.

Use PgBouncer

Connection pooling improves database performance by reusing existing connections rather than opening and closing new ones for each request. For this, install and configure PgBouncer on EC2:

- SSH into your EC2 instance using the private key and appropriate user (e.g., **`ec2-user`**).
- Update packages and install PgBouncer:

```
sudo yum update -y

sudo yum install -y pgbouncer
```

- Create a directory for PgBouncer configuration files:

```
mkdir ~/pgbouncer
```

- Create a configuration file (**`pgbouncer.ini`**) with the following content:

```
[databases]

adventureworks = host=<RDS_ENDPOINT> port=5432
dbname=adventureworks

[pgbouncer]

listen_addr = *

listen_port = 6432
```

```
auth_type = md5

auth_file = users.txt

logfile = pgbouncer.log

pidfile = pgbouncer.pid

admin_users = <MASTER_USERNAME>
```

- Replace **<RDS_ENDPOINT>** with your RDS endpoint and **<MASTER_USERNAME>** with your master username.
- Create a **users.txt** file in the same directory with the following content:

```
"<MASTER_USERNAME>" "<MASTER_PASSWORD>"
```

- Replace **<MASTER_USERNAME>** and **<MASTER_PASSWORD>** with your credentials.
- Launch PgBouncer using the configuration file:

```
pgbouncer ~/pgbouncer/pgbouncer.ini
```

- Update your application's connection string to use the PgBouncer instance, pointing to the EC2 instance's IP address and port **6432**.
- Adjust PgBouncer's connection limits and timeouts to optimize performance for your workload.

By following these steps, you effectively managed database connections to the AdventureWorks PostgreSQL database on AWS, ensuring a secure and high-performance setup that can handle demanding application workloads.

Recipe #5: Perform Replication of Database on AWS

This recipe focused on replicating the database using AWS RDS read replicas to enhance performance and ensure high availability.

Create a Read Replica

Before creating a read replica, automatic backups must be enabled for your RDS instance.

- In the RDS Dashboard, select your AdventureWorks database instance.
- Click "Modify" and scroll to the "Backup" section. Set the "Backup retention period" to a value greater than 0 (e.g., 7 days).

Read replicas help offload read traffic from the primary database, improving performance and scalability. To create Read Replica,

- In the RDS Dashboard, select the database instance and click "Actions," then choose "Create read replica."
- Provide a unique name for the replica instance and configure settings such as instance class, storage type, and network configuration.

Ensure the read replica's security group allows inbound traffic on port 5432, similar to the primary instance. To begin the replication,

- Click "Create read replica" to begin the replication process. AWS will handle the data synchronization automatically.
- Once the read replica is available, connect to it using a PostgreSQL client to verify data integrity.
- Use pgAdmin or **psql** to connect to the read replica instance:

```
psql --host=<READ_REPLICA_ENDPOINT> --port=5432 --
username=<MASTER_USERNAME> --password --
dbname=adventureworks
```

- Run queries to confirm that the data matches the primary database.

Monitor Replication Performance

- In the RDS Dashboard, select the read replica instance and view the "Monitoring" tab for the **ReplicaLag** metric. Here, try to aim for minimal lag to ensure up-to-date data.
- If needed, promote a read replica to a standalone RDS instance, useful in disaster recovery scenarios. For this, in the RDS Dashboard, select the read replica instance, click "Actions," and choose "Promote read replica." Then follow the prompts to complete the promotion, creating an independent RDS instance.

- If the read replica is no longer needed, delete it to save resources. For this, in the RDS Dashboard, select the read replica instance, click "Actions," and choose "Delete."

By implementing these steps, you successfully replicated the AdventureWorks database using AWS RDS read replicas, distributing read traffic and improving application performance.

Recipe #6: Run PostgreSQL Bi-directional Replication using pglogical

Bi-directional replication allows for multi-master replication between PostgreSQL databases, enabling changes to be replicated across multiple nodes. This setup is ideal for load balancing and high availability in distributed environments.

Install pglogical Extension

pglogical is a logical replication extension that supports bi-directional replication in PostgreSQL.

- In the RDS Dashboard, select both the primary and secondary instances.
- Click "Modify," then add **`pglogical`** to the **`shared_preload_libraries`** parameter under "Database options."
- Enable **`rds.logical_replication`** by setting it to **`1`**.
- Apply the changes immediately or during the next maintenance window.

Then, use a PostgreSQL client such as pgAdmin or **`psql`** to connect to both RDS instances with the master credentials. Then, run the following command to create the pglogical extension:

```
CREATE EXTENSION pglogical;
```

Configure Replication Nodes

Define unique node names and connection information for each instance.

- On the primary instance:

```
SELECT pglogical.create_node(
    node_name := 'adventureworks_primary_node',
```

```
    dsn := 'host=adventureworks_primary_endpoint port=5432
dbname=adventureworks user=<MASTER_USERNAME>
password=<MASTER_PASSWORD>'

);
```

- On the secondary instance:

```
SELECT pglogical.create_node(

    node_name := 'adventureworks_secondary_node',

    dsn := 'host=adventureworks_secondary_endpoint
port=5432 dbname=adventureworks user=<MASTER_USERNAME>
password=<MASTER_PASSWORD>'

);
```

- Replace the placeholders with the actual endpoint URLs, master username, and master password for your instances.
- Include all relevant tables and sequences in the replication set to ensure they are synchronized between instances.
- Add tables on both instances:

```
SELECT
pglogical.replication_set_add_all_tables('default',
ARRAY['public']);
```

- Add sequences on both instances:

```
SELECT
pglogical.replication_set_add_all_sequences('default',
ARRAY['public']);
```

Create Replication Subscriptions

- Establish subscriptions on each node to replicate changes bi-directionally. So, first on the primary instance:

```
SELECT pglogical.create_subscription(

    subscription_name :=
'adventureworks_primary_to_secondary',

    provider_dsn :=
'host=adventureworks_secondary_endpoint port=5432
dbname=adventureworks user=<MASTER_USERNAME>
password=<MASTER_PASSWORD>',

    replication_sets := ARRAY['default'],

    synchronize_structure := false,

    synchronize_data := true

);
```

- Now do it on the secondary instance:

```
SELECT pglogical.create_subscription(

    subscription_name :=
'adventureworks_secondary_to_primary',

    provider_dsn := 'host=adventureworks_primary_endpoint
port=5432 dbname=adventureworks user=<MASTER_USERNAME>
password=<MASTER_PASSWORD>',

    replication_sets := ARRAY['default'],

    synchronize_structure := false,

    synchronize_data := true

);
```

- Confirm that changes made on one instance are replicated to the other.
- To test the replication, Insert, update, or delete data in the AdventureWorks database on one instance and verify the changes appear on the other instance.
- And then run the following command on both instances to check the subscription status:

```
SELECT * FROM pglogical.show_subscription_status();
```

Make sure the status column shows 'replicating' for both subscriptions.

If replication issues occur, review PostgreSQL logs for errors or warnings related to pglogical:

- In the RDS Dashboard, navigate to "Logs & events" under the "Details" tab for each instance to review logs.
- Address any configuration or network issues that may be causing replication delays or failures.

By following these steps, you have successfully set up bi-directional replication for the database using pglogical, allowing you to distribute database load, improve performance, and ensure high availability in a distributed PostgreSQL environment. This configuration supports dynamic workloads and enhances your system's resilience against failures.

Summary

So overall in this chapter, you learned how to provision PostgreSQL databases in the cloud using AWS services, focusing on creating and managing PostgreSQL instances with Amazon RDS. You explored how to set up a PostgreSQL cloud instance, manage database connections with AWS EC2, and import the database for practical use. The chapter also covered performing backup and restore operations using native PostgreSQL tools, with a focus on safeguarding data integrity through Amazon S3 storage. You gained skills in creating backups with pg_dump, storing them securely, and restoring them when necessary.

Additionally, the chapter explored database replication strategies to improve performance and ensure high availability. You learned to utilize AWS RDS read replicas to offload read traffic and enhance scalability. You also explored bi-directional replication using the pglogical extension, allowing data synchronization across multiple PostgreSQL instances. By the end of this chapter, you had practical experience deploying and managing PostgreSQL databases in the cloud, using AWS tools to enhance performance, security, and availability.

Chapter 4: Database Migration to Cloud and PostgreSQL

Introduction

In this chapter, you will be exploring various methods of database migration to PostgreSQL, focusing on transitioning from on-premise systems to the cloud using AWS. You will be learning how to migrate the database from on-premise environments to AWS EC2 or RDS instances. This will involve creating database backups, transferring them securely to AWS, and restoring them on the new platform. You will also be understanding the benefits of cloud migration, including scalability, high availability, and the ability to leverage AWS services for monitoring and optimization.

You will be discovering the use of AWS Data Migration Service (DMS) to facilitate seamless database migration from an on-premise PostgreSQL server to an Amazon RDS for PostgreSQL instance. You will be learning how to configure source and target endpoints, create migration tasks, and monitor the migration process to ensure data integrity and consistency. Furthermore, you will be focusing on using **pgloader** to migrate databases from MySQL to PostgreSQL. You will be understanding how to set up and configure pgloader, create command files for data migration, and handle data type conversions during the process. Additionally, you will be exploring the setup and use of Foreign Data Wrappers (FDW) in PostgreSQL, allowing you to access and integrate data from remote databases seamlessly.

By the end of this chapter, you will have gained valuable knowledge and practical experience in migrating databases to PostgreSQL, using a range of tools and techniques to ensure smooth and efficient transitions.

Recipe #1: Migrating from On-Premise to AWS EC2/RDS Instance

This recipe walks you through migrating the database from an on-premise PostgreSQL server to an AWS EC2 or RDS instance, ensuring a smooth transition to a cloud environment.

Create Database Backup

Ensure your on-premise PostgreSQL server hosting the database is running and accessible. Then, obtain necessary credentials, including the username and password for your PostgreSQL server.

Followed by, use **pg_dump** to create a backup of the database:

```
pg_dump -U <USERNAME> -W -F t -f
adventureworks_backup.tar adventureworks
```

In this, replace **<USERNAME>** with your PostgreSQL username and enter your password when prompted. This command generates a tarball of the database.

Transfer Backup to AWS Environment

- If you haven't already, create an AWS account and sign in to the AWS Management Console. Create an EC2 or RDS instance for hosting the database. Refer to the steps in Chapter 3 for creating these instances.
- Then, transfer the **adventureworks_backup.tar** file to your AWS environment using one of the following methods:

Now for EC2 Instance, use SCP to transfer the backup file:

```
scp -i <PATH_TO_YOUR_PRIVATE_KEY>
adventureworks_backup.tar ec2-
user@<EC2_PUBLIC_DNS>:/home/ec2-user/
```

In this, replace **<PATH_TO_YOUR_PRIVATE_KEY>** with the path to your EC2 private key and **<EC2_PUBLIC_DNS>** with your EC2 instance's public DNS.

For RDS Instance, create an Amazon S3 bucket in the same region as your RDS instance. Then, upload the **adventureworks_backup.tar** file to the S3 bucket using the AWS Management Console or AWS CLI.

Verify Migration

- Install PostgreSQL on the EC2 instance if it isn't already set up, as shown in Chapter 3. Then, create an empty database:

```
createdb -U <USERNAME> -W adventureworks
```

- Restore the backup:

```
pg_restore -U <USERNAME> -W -d adventureworks
adventureworks_backup.tar
```

Here, if it is RDS Instances, create an empty database on your RDS instance using a PostgreSQL client such as pgAdmin or `psql`:

```
CREATE DATABASE adventureworks;
```

- Restore the backup using **pg_restore**:

```
pg_restore -h <RDS_ENDPOINT> -U <MASTER_USERNAME> -W -d
adventureworks adventureworks_backup.tar
```

In this, replace **<RDS_ENDPOINT>** and **<MASTER_USERNAME>** with your RDS instance's endpoint and master username.

You may run SQL queries to verify the tables, data, and other objects have been migrated correctly. By following these steps, you effectively migrated the database from an on-premise PostgreSQL server to an AWS EC2 or RDS instance, leveraging the scalability and high availability of AWS.

Recipe #2: Utilizing AWS Data Migration Service (DMS)

This recipe demonstrates how to migrate the AdventureWorks database from an on-premise PostgreSQL server to an Amazon RDS for PostgreSQL instance using AWS Data Migration Service (DMS).

Setup AWS Environment

- Ensure your on-premise PostgreSQL server is running and accessible with the necessary credentials.
- Create an Amazon RDS for PostgreSQL instance to host the database, as explained in Chapter 3.
- If your on-premise PostgreSQL server is hosted in an Amazon VPC, create a VPC peering connection between the VPC hosting your on-premise server and the VPC hosting the RDS instance:
- In the AWS Management Console, navigate to the VPC Dashboard.
- Click on "Peering Connections" and create a new connection, specifying the VPC IDs for both the requester and accepter VPCs. And, accept the peering connection request on the accepter VPC side.

Create Endpoints in AWS DMS Replication Instance

- In the AWS Management Console, navigate to the DMS Dashboard. Click on "Replication instances" and create a new replication instance. Provide a name, description, instance class, and allocated storage. Select the VPC containing your on-premise PostgreSQL server and RDS instance.

- In the DMS Dashboard, click on "Endpoints" and create endpoints for both the source and target databases. Provide an endpoint identifier, select PostgreSQL as the source engine, and enter the connection details for your on-premise server. Also, similarly provide an endpoint identifier for the target engine, and enter the connection details for your RDS instance.
- Test the source and target endpoints in the DMS Dashboard to ensure successful connections.

Create Database Migration Task

- In the DMS Dashboard,
    - click on "Database migration tasks" and create a new migration task.
    - provide a name, description, replication instance, source and target endpoints, and choose the migration type.
    - configure task settings, such as logging, and define table mappings for the database.
- Start the migration task and monitor its progress in the DMS Dashboard. Ensure data is transferred successfully without errors.

By utilizing AWS DMS, you successfully migrated the database to an Amazon RDS for PostgreSQL instance, minimizing downtime and benefiting from AWS's robust services.

Recipe #3: Migrating Database from EC2 to RDS Instance

This recipe focuses on migrating the database from an Amazon EC2 instance to an Amazon RDS instance, allowing you to leverage RDS's managed features.

Create Backup of Database

- Ensure your EC2 instance hosting the PostgreSQL server is running and accessible with the necessary credentials. Use **pg_dump** to create a backup on the EC2 instance:

```
pg_dump -U <USERNAME> -W -F t -f
adventureworks_backup.tar adventureworks
```

- Replace **<USERNAME>** with your PostgreSQL username and enter the password.
- Create an Amazon RDS for PostgreSQL instance as detailed in previous chapters.
- Upload the **adventureworks_backup.tar** file to an Amazon S3 bucket in the same region as your RDS instance.
- Create an IAM role granting your RDS instance permission to access the S3 bucket:
- In the IAM Dashboard,
    - create a new role for the RDS service.
    - Attach the "AmazonS3ReadOnlyAccess" policy to the role.
    - Modify your RDS instance to use this IAM role for S3 import/export.

Restore Database

- Create an empty database on your RDS instance using pgAdmin or **psql**:

```
CREATE DATABASE adventureworks;
```

- Use the AWS CLI to execute the **aws rds restore-db-instance-from-s3** command to restore the backup:

```
aws rds restore-db-instance-from-s3 \
  --db-instance-identifier <RDS_INSTANCE_IDENTIFIER> \
  --db-instance-class <RDS_INSTANCE_CLASS> \
  --engine postgres \
  --master-username <MASTER_USERNAME> \
  --master-user-password <MASTER_USER_PASSWORD> \
  --vpc-security-group-ids <VPC_SECURITY_GROUP_ID> \
  --s3-bucket-name <BUCKET_NAME> \
  --s3-prefix adventureworks_backup.tar \
  --source-engine postgres \
```

```
--source-engine-version <SOURCE_ENGINE_VERSION> \
--region <AWS_REGION> \
--availability-zone <AVAILABILITY_ZONE> \
--db-name adventureworks \
--backup-retention-period 7
```

- Replace the placeholders with your specific values:
    - **`<RDS_INSTANCE_IDENTIFIER>`**: A unique name for the new RDS instance.
    - **`<RDS_INSTANCE_CLASS>`**: The instance class for the RDS instance (e.g., **`db.t2.micro`**).
    - **`<MASTER_USERNAME>`**: The master username for the RDS instance.
    - **`<MASTER_USER_PASSWORD>`**: The master user password for the RDS instance.
    - **`<VPC_SECURITY_GROUP_ID>`**: The VPC security group ID for the RDS instance.
    - **`<BUCKET_NAME>`**: The name of the S3 bucket containing the backup file.
    - **`<SOURCE_ENGINE_VERSION>`**: The PostgreSQL version used on your EC2 instance (e.g., **`13.3`**).
    - **`<AWS_REGION>`**: The AWS region where the RDS instance is located (e.g., **`us-west-2`**).
    - **`<AVAILABILITY_ZONE>`**: The availability zone for the RDS instance (e.g., **`us-west-2a`**).

After this, run SQL queries to verify that the tables, data, and other objects have been migrated correctly and ensure the data integrity of the database.

Monitor and Optimize

Monitor the performance and resource usage of your RDS instance using Amazon CloudWatch, setting up alerts for specific events. Depending on your findings, consider:

- Scaling the RDS instance vertically by increasing the instance size (CPU, memory, and storage).

- Optimizing PostgreSQL configuration parameters for better performance, such as **shared_buffers**, **effective_cache_size**, and **maintenance_work_mem**.
- Analyzing and optimizing slow-running queries using the **EXPLAIN** command or other query profiling tools.
- Implementing caching, indexing, and partitioning strategies to improve database performance.

By completing these steps, you have successfully migrated the database from an Amazon EC2 instance to an Amazon RDS instance. This migration process allows you to take advantage of RDS's managed features, such as automatic backups, patching, and high availability.

Recipe #4: Preparing Pgloader to Use with Database

In this recipe, you'll learn how to prepare and use **pgloader**, a powerful open-source data migration tool, to migrate data into PostgreSQL.

Install Pgloader

- First, update package list:

```
sudo apt-get update
```

- Install Pgloader:

```
sudo apt-get install -y pgloader
```

Pgloader is now installed on your system and ready for use. Then, confirm that pgloader is installed correctly by checking its version:

```
pgloader --version
```

You should then see the pgloader version number, confirming the installation.

Create Pgloader Command File

- Ensure both your source database (e.g., MySQL, SQL Server, or SQLite) and target PostgreSQL database are running and accessible. And, also confirm you have the necessary credentials for both databases.
- Then, create a command file to define the migration process, including connection details and data transformations:

```
nano pgloader_command_file.load
```

- Add the following contents to the command file:

```
LOAD DATABASE

    FROM <SOURCE_DB_CONNECTION_STRING>

    INTO <TARGET_DB_CONNECTION_STRING>


WITH include drop create tables create indexes reset
sequences

     data only


SET maintenance_work_mem to '128MB', work_mem to '12MB',
search_path to 'public'

CAST type <SOURCE_TYPE> to <TARGET_TYPE> drop typemod


BEFORE LOAD DO

$$ create schema if not exists public; $$;
```

- Replace **<SOURCE_DB_CONNECTION_STRING>** and **<TARGET_DB_CONNECTION_STRING>** with your actual connection strings.

Specify any type casting needed for source and target data types using **<SOURCE_TYPE>** and **<TARGET_TYPE>**.

- Execute the pgloader command file to start the migration process:

```
pgloader pgloader_command_file.load
```

After the migration, connect to the PostgreSQL database using **psql** or **pgAdmin** and run SQL queries to verify the data integrity and ensure that tables and other objects are correctly migrated.

These above steps establish pgloader and uses it to migrate data into PostgreSQL, streamlining the migration process with automatic schema and data type conversions.

Recipe #5: Migrating from MySQL to PostgreSQL

In this recipe, you'll migrate the database from MySQL to PostgreSQL using **pgloader**, leveraging its robust capabilities for seamless data migration.

Create Pgloader Command File

- Ensure that your MySQL server hosting the database is running and accessible. Obtain the necessary credentials for both databases.
- Follow the installation steps in Recipe #4 to install pgloader if not already done.
- Create a command file named **mysql_to_postgresql.load**:

```
nano mysql_to_postgresql.load
```

- Add the following content:

```
LOAD DATABASE

   FROM
mysql://<MYSQL_USERNAME>:<MYSQL_PASSWORD>@<MYSQL_HOST>:<M
YSQL_PORT>/adventureworks
```

```
    INTO
postgresql://<POSTGRESQL_USERNAME>:<POSTGRESQL_PASSWORD>@
<POSTGRESQL_HOST>:<POSTGRESQL_PORT>/adventureworks

WITH include drop create tables create indexes reset
sequences

     data only


SET maintenance_work_mem to '128MB', work_mem to '12MB',
search_path to 'public'


CAST type datetime to timestamptz drop typemod

     type date drop not null using zero-dates-to-null

     type tinyint to smallint


BEFORE LOAD DO

$$ create schema if not exists public; $$;
```

- Replace placeholders with your actual MySQL and PostgreSQL credentials and connection details.

Run the Migration

- Execute the pgloader command file to start the migration:

```
pgloader mysql_to_postgresql.load
```

- Monitor the terminal output for progress and any potential issues.

- Connect to the database using **psql** or **pgAdmin** and verify the data integrity by running SQL queries to ensure that tables and other objects have been migrated correctly.

By adhering to these procedures, you have accomplished the database migration from MySQL to PostgreSQL with the help of pgloader. The migration was smooth because it addressed issues with data type conversions and application adjustments.

Recipe #6: Setting up Foreign Data Wrapper (FDW)

In this recipe, you'll learn how to set up a FDW to access and manipulate data stored in remote databases, facilitating data integration.

Install MySQL FDW

PostgreSQL supports various FDWs for accessing different database systems. To access a MySQL database,

- You'll need to install the **mysql_fdw** extension.

```
sudo apt-get install postgresql-contrib-13
libmysqlclient-dev

sudo apt-get install postgresql-13-mysql-fdw
```

- Define a server object specifying connection parameters and options for the remote data source:

```
CREATE SERVER mysql_server

FOREIGN DATA WRAPPER mysql_fdw

OPTIONS (host 'mysql.gitforgits.com', port '3306', dbname
'adventureworks');
```

- Replace the placeholders with your actual MySQL server details. Define user credentials for accessing the remote data source:

```
CREATE USER MAPPING FOR postgres
```

```
SERVER mysql_server
OPTIONS (username 'user', password 'password');
```

- Replace the placeholders with your MySQL username and password.

Create FDW Table

- Define a table object that maps to a remote table in the FDW server:

```
CREATE FOREIGN TABLE salesorderheader (
  salesorderid integer,
  revisionnumber integer,
  orderdate date,
  duedate date,
  shipdate date,
  status integer,
  onlineorderflag boolean,
  salesordernumber varchar,
  purchaseordernumber varchar,
  accountnumber varchar,
  customerid integer,
  salespersonid integer,
  territoryid integer,
  billtoaddressid integer,  shiptoaddressid integer,
  shipmethodid integer,
```

```
  creditcardid integer,
  creditcardapprovalcode varchar,
  currencyrateid integer,
  subtotal numeric(12,2),
  taxamt numeric(12,2),
  freight numeric(12,2),
  totaldue numeric(12,2),
  comment text
)
SERVER mysql_server
OPTIONS (schema_name 'sales', table_name
'salesorderheader');
```

- Then, adjust the column definitions to match your MySQL schema and replace the placeholders with your actual MySQL schema and table names.
- After this, use a SQL command to migrate data from the FDW table to a native PostgreSQL table:

```
INSERT INTO postgres_salesorderheader
SELECT * FROM salesorderheader;
```

- Then, replace **postgres_salesorderheader** with the name of the target PostgreSQL table.

These steps sets up a Foreign Data Wrapper (FDW) in PostgreSQL. This will allow you to integrate data from a remote database, making it easier to access and migrate to PostgreSQL.

Summary

Overall, here you learned about different methods for migrating databases to PostgreSQL, focusing on the transition from on-premise systems to AWS. You explored how to migrate the database from on-premise environments to AWS EC2 or RDS instances, including creating backups, transferring them securely, and restoring them on the cloud. The chapter highlighted the benefits of cloud migration, such as scalability and high availability. Additionally, you discovered the use of AWS Data Migration Service (DMS) to facilitate seamless database migration, minimizing downtime and ensuring data integrity. You learned to configure source and target endpoints, create migration tasks, and monitor the migration process.

This chapter also covered using pgloader to migrate databases from MySQL to PostgreSQL, focusing on setup, configuration, and data type conversion. Furthermore, you explored setting up Foreign Data Wrappers (FDW) to access and integrate data from remote databases. This detailed learning experience equipped you with the skills needed for efficient database migration and integration in modern cloud environments.

CHAPTER 5: WAL, AUTOVACUUM & ARCHIVELOG

Introduction

In this chapter, you will be exploring advanced PostgreSQL features related to Write-Ahead Logging (WAL) and the vacuum process. You will be learning how to manage WAL files efficiently by enabling compression to save disk space and reduce I/O operations. This will involve configuring PostgreSQL settings to optimize performance and monitor WAL activity. Understanding these techniques will help you maintain a healthy database environment, especially for large databases like AdventureWorks. Additionally, you will be focusing on remote WAL archiving, an essential practice for disaster recovery and high availability. You will be discovering how to configure PostgreSQL to archive WAL files to a remote server, ensuring data durability in case of server failures. This includes setting up secure transfers using SSH keys and implementing retention policies to manage archive storage effectively. By mastering these techniques, you will enhance your database's resilience and recoverability.

Furthermore, you will be diving into the vacuum process, a critical maintenance task that reclaims storage space and improves query performance. You will learn how to execute **VACUUM** and **VACUUM FULL** operations, analyze their impact on query performance, and configure autovacuum settings for automated maintenance. You will also explore debugging strategies to address autovacuum issues, ensuring that your database remains optimized for performance and storage efficiency. This chapter will equip you to maintain high-performance databases with robust disaster recovery capabilities in diverse environments.

Recipe #1: WAL Compression Option for Space Management

In this recipe, you will learn how to enable WAL (Write-Ahead Logging) compression to manage storage space efficiently. WAL compression helps reduce the size of WAL files by compressing the data portion of WAL records, which is particularly beneficial for large databases like AdventureWorks.

Enable WALCompression

Use the **SHOW data_directory;** command to find the location of the **postgresql.conf** configuration file, where you will enable WAL compression. Navigate to the PostgreSQL data directory:

```
cd /var/lib/postgresql/13/main  # Example path; adjust
based on your setup
```

Use a text editor to open **postgresql.conf**:

```
sudo nano postgresql.conf
```

Find the **wal_compression** parameter in the configuration file. If it is commented out (indicated by a **#**), uncomment it and set its value to **on**:

```
wal_compression = on
```

Tune WAL Compression

When WAL compression is enabled, PostgreSQL compresses the main data portion of WAL records using a lightweight compression algorithm. This helps reduce the amount of disk space required for storing WAL files and can also lower I/O operations, improving overall system performance.

After enabling WAL compression, restart the PostgreSQL service to apply the changes:

```
sudo systemctl restart postgresql
```

Confirm that WAL compression is enabled by checking the PostgreSQL logs and monitoring WAL file sizes:

```
ls -lh /var/lib/postgresql/13/main/pg_wal  # Check the
size of WAL files
```

If needed, adjust other WAL-related parameters such as **wal_buffers** and **checkpoint_timeout** to optimize performance further:

```
wal_buffers = 16MB

checkpoint_timeout = 10min
```

These steps allowed you to enable PostgreSQL's WAL compression, which decreased the amount of storage space needed for WAL files and enhanced write performance. Managing disk usage is especially important for large databases such as AdventureWorks, where this setup comes in handy.

Recipe #2: Configure WAL Performance Parameters

In this recipe, you will learn how to configure various WAL performance parameters to optimize write performance, recovery time, and replication lag. These settings play a critical role in maintaining the efficiency and reliability of your PostgreSQL database.

Adjust WAL Performance Parameters

As before, use **`SHOW data_directory;`** to find the **`postgresql.conf`** file and navigate to the data directory.

Use a text editor to open **`postgresql.conf`**:

```
sudo nano postgresql.conf
```

Then, modify the following key WAL parameters to optimize performance:

- wal_level

Determines the level of detail in WAL records. Higher levels log more information, which is required for certain features like logical replication and PITR.

```
wal_level = replica  # Default setting, suitable for most
use cases
```

- wal_buffers

Specifies the amount of shared memory allocated for WAL data. Increasing this value can improve write performance.

```
wal_buffers = 16MB
```

- checkpoint_timeout

Defines the maximum time between automatic checkpoints. Longer intervals reduce checkpoint frequency, improving write performance but increasing recovery time.

```
checkpoint_timeout = 10min
```

- max_wal_size

Sets the maximum amount of WAL data between checkpoints. Higher values can enhance performance but may extend recovery time.

```
max_wal_size = 2GB
```

- min_wal_size

Defines the minimum amount of WAL space reserved, helping prevent WAL space exhaustion during high-load periods.

```
min_wal_size = 128MB
```

- synchronous_commit

Controls whether transaction commits wait for WAL records to be flushed to disk. Disabling this can improve write performance but risks data loss in crashes.

```
synchronous_commit = off  # Use with caution; may lead to
data loss
```

Save the changes to **postgresql.conf** and restart PostgreSQL to apply the new settings:

```
sudo systemctl restart postgresql
```

Monitor WAL Performance

Use PostgreSQL's built-in views to monitor WAL performance and replication lag:

```
SELECT client_addr, pg_xlog_location_diff(sent_location,
replay_location) AS replication_lag

FROM pg_stat_replication;

SELECT archived_count, last_archived_wal,

last_archived_time

FROM pg_stat_archiver;
```

```
SELECT checkpoints_timed, checkpoints_req,
buffers_checkpoint, buffers_clean, buffers_backend

FROM pg_stat_bgwriter;
```

Evaluate Impact and Fine-Tune Settings

Analyze the results of your configuration changes and adjust parameters as needed to achieve optimal performance. Consider running benchmarks and monitoring system metrics over time to understand the effects. After this, perform operations on the database, such as batch inserts or updates, to evaluate how the new settings impact performance and WAL generation:

```
INSERT INTO sales.orders (customer_id, order_date,
total_due)

SELECT customer_id, CURRENT_DATE, total_due

FROM sales.orders

WHERE order_date = CURRENT_DATE - INTERVAL '1 day';
```

By configuring WAL performance parameters, you optimized PostgreSQL for better write throughput and managed recovery and replication considerations effectively, enhancing the performance and reliability of the database.

Recipe #3: Administer Continuous Archiving

Continuous Archiving allows for continuous backup of WAL files to a separate storage location, enabling Point-In-Time Recovery (PITR) and supporting replication scenarios. In this recipe, you will learn how to set up and administer continuous archiving.

Test Archiving Setup

Use the **SHOW data_directory;** command to find the **postgresql.conf** file and open it for editing:

```
sudo nano postgresql.conf
```

Set the **archive_command** parameter to specify how WAL files should be archived. This command copies WAL files to a designated archive destination:

```
archive_command = 'rsync %p
user@remotehost:/path/to/archive/%f'
```

Replace **user@remotehost:/path/to/archive/** with your remote server details and archive directory path. Ensure SSH access is set up for secure transfers. Then, turn on the **archive_mode** parameter to start archiving WAL files:

```
archive_mode = on
```

PostgreSQL 15 also supports multiple archive destinations for redundancy or load balancing. You can use the **archive_destinations** parameter:

```
archive_destinations = '/local/archive/path,
user@remotehost:/remote/archive/path'
```

Apply the configuration changes:

```
sudo systemctl restart postgresql
```

Create a checkpoint and verify that WAL files are archived correctly:

```
SELECT pg_create_checkpoint();
```

Check the specified archive destination(s) to confirm that the WAL file has been successfully copied. Use PostgreSQL system views to monitor the status and progress of WAL archiving:

```
SELECT * FROM pg_stat_archiver;
```

This query provides information about the number of WAL files archived, the last archived file, and any pending files.

Manage Archive Retention and Cleanup

Implement a retention policy to manage archived WAL files and free up disk space as needed.

Use the **find** command to identify old WAL files in the archive directory:

```
find /path/to/archive -type f -mtime +30
```

This command lists files older than 30 days, allowing you to assess which files can be safely deleted. Remove identified files to reclaim storage space:

```
find /path/to/archive -type f -mtime +30 -delete
```

Prepare Recovery Environment

Set up a recovery instance and configure the **recovery.conf** file with appropriate parameters for PITR:

```
restore_command = 'cp /path/to/archive/%f %p'

recovery_target_time = '2023-08-01 12:00:00'
```

Start the PostgreSQL server in recovery mode to apply archived WAL files and restore the database to the desired state. And, also check that the database state matches the expected results by querying tables and validating data integrity.

Recipe #4: Using Remote WAL Archive Options

Remote WAL archiving involves transferring Write-Ahead Log (WAL) files from the primary PostgreSQL server to a remote location, ensuring that you can recover data in case of failures. In this recipe, you'll learn how to set up and manage remote WAL archiving effectively.

Setup SSH Keys for Secure Transfer:

The **archive_command** parameter in the **postgresql.conf** file specifies how to copy WAL files to a remote server. Open the **postgresql.conf** file:

```
sudo nano /var/lib/postgresql/13/main/postgresql.conf
```

Set the **archive_command** parameter to use **rsync** for remote copying:

```
archive_command = 'rsync %p
user@192.0.2.1:/path/to/archive/%f'
```

Replace **user@192.0.2.1** with the username and IP address of your remote server and **/path/to/archive/** with the desired archive directory on the remote server.

Then, generate an SSH key pair on the primary server:

```
ssh-keygen -t rsa
```

Copy the public key to the remote server:

```
ssh-copy-id user@192.0.2.1
```

Verify SSH access without a password:

```
ssh user@192.0.2.1
```

To reduce network traffic, enable compression in the **archive_command** by adding the **-z** option:

```
archive_command = 'rsync -z %p
user@192.0.2.1:/path/to/archive/%f'
```

Enable Archive Mode:

Ensure **archive_mode** is set to **on** in the **postgresql.conf** file:

```
archive_mode = on
```

Apply the configuration changes:

```
sudo systemctl restart postgresql
```

Create a new database and insert data to generate WAL activity:

```
CREATE DATABASE test_db;

INSERT INTO sales.orders (customer_id, order_date,
total_due) VALUES (101, CURRENT_DATE, 250.75);
```

Create a checkpoint to trigger WAL archiving:

```
SELECT pg_create_checkpoint();
```

Archived WAL Files on Remote Server

Log into the remote server and check the archive directory for the presence of new WAL files:

```
ls /path/to/archive/
```

Use the **pg_stat_archiver** view to monitor archiving status:

```
SELECT archived_count, last_archived_wal,
last_archived_time FROM pg_stat_archiver;
```

Check PostgreSQL logs for any errors related to archiving and ensure network connectivity between the primary and remote servers. You may also setup a cron job on the remote server to delete older WAL files based on your retention policy:

```
find /path/to/archive -type f -mtime +30 -delete
```

By setting up remote WAL archiving, you enhance the disaster recovery capabilities of your PostgreSQL server, as this configuration allows you to securely transfer and store WAL files on a remote server.

Recipe #5: Exploring Vacuum Process

The **VACUUM** process is essential for maintaining database health by reclaiming storage space and improving query performance. This process removes dead rows left by updates and deletes, ensuring efficient storage usage. In this recipe, you'll learn how to perform and optimize the **VACUUM** process on the database.

Perform a Basic VACUUM

The **VACUUM** process reclaims storage space by removing dead tuples (rows) from tables and indexes. It also updates the visibility map for efficient query planning. Also, regular vacuuming prevents bloat, which can degrade performance over time.

Now, connect to the database using **psql**:

```
psql -d adventureworks
```

Run the **VACUUM** command to clean up a specific table:

```
VACUUM sales.orders;
```

Execute VACUUM FULL

VACUUM FULL performs a more thorough cleanup, reclaiming additional space by rewriting the entire table. Note that this locks the table during execution. Run **VACUUM FULL** on a table:

```
VACUUM FULL sales.orders;
```

Use **VACUUM FULL** sparingly, ideally during maintenance windows, as it requires exclusive locks on tables.

Use **EXPLAIN ANALYZE** to compare query performance before and after vacuuming:

```
EXPLAIN ANALYZE SELECT * FROM sales.orders WHERE
total_due > 500;
```

Automate VACUUM

PostgreSQL's **autovacuum** process automatically triggers vacuuming based on table activity and thresholds.

Check autovacuum settings:

```
SHOW autovacuum;
```

Adjust autovacuum parameters in **postgresql.conf** if necessary:

```
autovacuum_vacuum_scale_factor = 0.1  # Vacuum when 10

 of a table has been modified

autovacuum_analyze_scale_factor = 0.05  # Analyze when 5%
of a table has been modified
```

Use system views to monitor vacuum activity and assess table health:

```
SELECT relname, last_vacuum, last_autovacuum, n_dead_tup
FROM pg_stat_user_tables
WHERE n_dead_tup > 1000;
```

Handle Large Tables

For very large tables, consider partitioning to improve vacuum efficiency. This divides tables into smaller, manageable segments. For this, create a partitioned table:

```
CREATE TABLE sales.orders_part (
  order_id INT,
  order_date DATE,
  total_due NUMERIC
) PARTITION BY RANGE (order_date);
```

Optimize and Run VACUUM in Parallel

Adjust **maintenance_work_mem** and **vacuum_cost_limit** parameters for better vacuum performance:

```
maintenance_work_mem = 256MB
vacuum_cost_limit = 2000
```

Utilize parallel vacuuming to enhance performance, especially for large databases:

```
VACUUM (PARALLEL 2) sales.orders;
```

Check logs for vacuum-related messages and inspect any anomalies or performance bottlenecks. By exploring and optimizing the **VACUUM** process, you ensured efficient storage management and improved query performance. Regular vacuuming and autovacuum configuration helps to maintain a healthy PostgreSQL environment.

Recipe #6: Debug PostgreSQL Autovacuum

The **autovacuum** process automatically maintains database health by reclaiming space and updating statistics. However, it may sometimes fail to perform as expected, leading to performance issues. In this recipe, you'll learn how to debug and optimize the **autovacuum** process for the AdventureWorks database.

Check Autovacuum Settings

autovacuum automatically vacuums and analyzes tables based on activity and predefined thresholds. It helps maintain performance by preventing table bloat.

Verify current autovacuum settings using SQL queries:

```
SELECT name, setting FROM pg_settings WHERE name LIKE
'autovacuum%';
```

Ensure settings align with your workload and database size. Adjust parameters in **postgresql.conf** if needed.

Review Autovacuum Logs and Manually Trigger

Check PostgreSQL logs for autovacuum-related messages, which provide insights into its operation and any issues:

```
sudo tail -f /var/log/postgresql/postgresql-13-main.log
```

Look for messages indicating skipped or delayed vacuum operations. Use system views to identify tables with high dead tuple counts and assess vacuum needs:

```
SELECT relname, n_dead_tup, last_autovacuum

FROM pg_stat_user_tables

WHERE n_dead_tup > 1000;
```

This query helps identify tables that may require more frequent vacuuming. If autovacuum is not keeping up, manually vacuum problematic tables:

```
VACUUM ANALYZE sales.orders;
```

This command performs both a vacuum and an analyze, updating table statistics for the query planner.

Adjust Autovacuum Settings

If necessary, adjust autovacuum settings in **postgresql.conf** for more aggressive vacuuming. Reduces the threshold of dead rows before vacuuming triggers. Set to a lower value for more frequent vacuuming:

```
autovacuum_vacuum_scale_factor = 0.05  # Vacuum when 5%
of a table is modified
```

Similar to vacuum scale factor, but for analyzing tables you set lower for more frequent analysis:

```
autovacuum_analyze_scale_factor = 0.02  # Analyze when 2%
of a table is modified

autovacuum_max_workers = 5
```

Check the **pg_stat_activity** view for active autovacuum processes:

```
SELECT pid, datname, relname, query, state

FROM pg_stat_activity

WHERE query LIKE '%autovacuum%';
```

For large tables, partitioning can improve autovacuum efficiency by reducing the number of rows processed at a time. This helps the autovacuum process keep up with data changes.

Adjust Cost-Based Vacuum Parameters

Tune cost-based vacuum parameters to balance system load and vacuum performance:

- vacuum_cost_delay

Specifies the delay between vacuum operations. Reduce the delay for more aggressive vacuuming:

```
vacuum_cost_delay = 0  # Disable delay for more
aggressive vacuuming
```

- vacuum_cost_limit

Sets the maximum cost for vacuum operations before a delay is enforced. Increase the limit to allow more work:

```
vacuum_cost_limit = 2000
```

After adjustments, monitor system performance and query execution times to ensure autovacuum is performing optimally. Fine-tune settings as necessary to achieve the desired balance between performance and resource usage. By effectively debugging and optimizing the **autovacuum** process, you ensured efficient space reclamation and improved query performance for the database.

Summary

Overall, you learned about advanced PostgreSQL features related to Write-Ahead Logging (WAL) and vacuum processes. You explored how to manage WAL files efficiently by enabling compression, which helped save disk space and reduce I/O operations. You configured PostgreSQL settings to optimize performance and monitored WAL activity to maintain a healthy database environment, especially for large databases like AdventureWorks. The chapter also covered remote WAL archiving, teaching you how to configure PostgreSQL to archive WAL files to a remote server for disaster recovery and high availability. You set up secure transfers using SSH keys and implemented retention policies to manage archive storage effectively. These techniques enhanced the database's resilience and recoverability.

Additionally, you delved into the vacuum process, learning to execute VACUUM and VACUUM FULL operations to reclaim storage space and improve query performance. You configured autovacuum settings for automated maintenance and explored debugging strategies to address autovacuum issues. This ensured your databases remained optimized for performance and storage efficiency.

Overall, this chapter provided you with a detailed understanding of WAL management, remote archiving, and vacuum processes, equipping you to maintain high-performance databases with robust disaster recovery capabilities and ensure data integrity and availability in diverse environments.

CHAPTER 6: PARTITIONING AND SHARDING STRATEGIES

Introduction

This chapter will cover advanced PostgreSQL partitioning and sharding techniques that can be used to efficiently manage and optimize large datasets. In this chapter, you will discover declarative methods for setting up partitioning, which streamline data management through the automatic distribution of data across partitions according to predefined criteria. Large tables, such as those in the AdventureWorks database, will be easier to manage with this strategy, which will also improve query performance. Additionally, you will learn how to dynamically manage partitions by attaching, releasing, and attaching them again as needed. These methods will provide you the adaptability you need to effectively manage requirements for archiving and data growth. You will be able to maximize storage and performance while preserving data integrity if you know how to manage partitions over time.

To further distribute data across multiple nodes, you will also be concentrating on sharding strategies with tools such as CitusData and FWD. By doing this, you'll be able to expand the AdventureWorks database horizontally, which will help it manage bigger datasets and function better overall. Implementing sharding will teach you how to guarantee high availability, improve query processing capabilities, and distribute load evenly among shards. Your ability to manage massive datasets and optimize your database for performance and scalability in varied environments will be greatly enhanced once you finish this chapter and acquire a thorough grasp of PostgreSQL's partitioning and sharding strategies.

Recipe #1: Setup Partitioning

Partitioning is a critical technique for improving query performance and managing large tables by dividing them into smaller, more manageable partitions. This recipe will walk you through setting up partitioning for the AdventureWorks database, demonstrating how to optimize performance and storage efficiency.

Define Partitions

PostgreSQL supports several partitioning strategies: **Range Partitioning**, **List Partitioning**, and **Hash Partitioning**. **Range Partitioning** is suitable for data that is continuous, such as dates or numeric ranges. **List Partitioning** is ideal for discrete values, like categories or states. **Hash Partitioning** evenly distributes data across partitions based on a hash function, which is useful for balancing load across partitions.

For the database, we will use **Range Partitioning** on the **`orders`** table, partitioning by **`order_date`**. This strategy will help optimize queries based on time intervals, which are common in reporting and analysis.

Next, use the **`CREATE TABLE`** statement with the **`PARTITION BY`** clause to create a partitioned table:

```
CREATE TABLE orders (
  id SERIAL PRIMARY KEY,
  order_date DATE NOT NULL,
  customer_id INTEGER NOT NULL,
  total_due NUMERIC(12, 2)
)
PARTITION BY RANGE (order_date);
```

This command creates a partitioned **orders** table with **order_date** as the partition key, using range partitioning. Create individual partitions for specific date ranges using the **CREATE TABLE ... PARTITION OF** command:

```
CREATE TABLE orders_2023 PARTITION OF orders
FOR VALUES FROM ('2023-01-01') TO ('2024-01-01');


CREATE TABLE orders_2024 PARTITION OF orders
FOR VALUES FROM ('2024-01-01') TO ('2025-01-01');
```

These commands create partitions for orders placed in the years 2023 and 2024.

Monitor Partition Usage and Performance

Create indexes on partitions to enhance query performance. You can create indexes on each partition separately or on the partitioned table as a whole:

```
CREATE INDEX orders_2023_customer_id_idx ON orders_2023
(customer_id);
```

This index optimizes queries that filter by **customer_id** within the 2023 partition.

Insert data into the partitioned table as usual, and PostgreSQL will automatically route the data to the correct partition based on the **order_date**:

```
INSERT INTO orders (order_date, customer_id, total_due)

VALUES ('2023-05-15', 123, 150.00);
```

Consider using tools like **pg_repack** to reclaim storage space and reorganize data within partitions if necessary. Use PostgreSQL system views to monitor partition usage and query performance:

```
SELECT relname, n_tup_ins, n_tup_upd, n_tup_del

FROM pg_stat_user_tables

WHERE relname LIKE 'orders%';
```

Partitioning can significantly improve query performance and manageability for large tables, but it requires careful planning and ongoing maintenance. By following these steps, you set up partitioning for the database, optimizing the **orders** table for efficient query performance and storage management.

Recipe #2: Vertical & Horizontal Partitioning

Beyond traditional partitioning, PostgreSQL supports vertical and horizontal partitioning, offering further flexibility in data organization and query performance. **Vertical Partitioning** involves splitting a table into multiple tables based on columns, allowing you to isolate frequently accessed or large data columns for improved performance. Whereas, **Horizontal Partitioning** involves dividing a table into multiple tables based on rows, typically using techniques similar to standard partitioning strategies.

This recipe will explore these techniques, demonstrating how to apply them to the AdventureWorks database.

Implement Vertical Partitioning

Consider vertical partitioning for the **orders** table, where the **order_details** column contains large data that is infrequently accessed. Create separate tables for frequently and infrequently accessed columns:

```
CREATE TABLE orders_base (
  id SERIAL PRIMARY KEY,
  order_date DATE NOT NULL,
  customer_id INTEGER NOT NULL
);

CREATE TABLE order_details (
  id SERIAL PRIMARY KEY,
  order_id INTEGER REFERENCES orders_base(id),
  details JSONB NOT NULL
);
```

This setup allows efficient access to **orders_base** while isolating **order_details**. Use **JOIN** operations to access data across vertically partitioned tables:

```
SELECT o.id, o.order_date, od.details
FROM orders_base o
JOIN order_details od ON o.id = od.order_id
WHERE o.customer_id = 123;
```

Implement Horizontal Partitioning

Horizontal partitioning is similar to range partitioning, where you divide tables into row-based partitions. For the **orders** table, implement horizontal partitioning by order year:

```
CREATE TABLE orders_2022 (
```

```
  CHECK (order_date >= '2022-01-01' AND order_date <
'2023-01-01')

) INHERITS (orders_base);


CREATE TABLE orders_2023 (

  CHECK (order_date >= '2023-01-01' AND order_date <
'2024-01-01')

) INHERITS (orders_base);
```

Each child table inherits the structure of **`orders_base`** and contains a subset of rows. Insert data into specific partitions to ensure efficient routing and access:

```
INSERT INTO orders_2023 (order_date, customer_id)

VALUES ('2023-06-01', 456);
```

Query the parent table, and PostgreSQL will automatically route queries to the appropriate partition based on constraints:

```
SELECT * FROM orders_base WHERE order_date BETWEEN '2023-
01-01' AND '2023-12-31';
```

Regularly optimize both vertically and horizontally partitioned tables to ensure efficient storage and query performance using **VACUUM** and **ANALYZE**:

```
VACUUM ANALYZE orders_2023;
```

Use system views to assess partition effectiveness and query performance, adjusting partitioning strategies as needed:

```
SELECT relname, n_tup_ins, n_tup_upd, n_tup_del

FROM pg_stat_user_tables
```

```
WHERE relname LIKE 'orders%';
```

Vertical partitioning is ideal for separating large, infrequently accessed data from frequently accessed data. Horizontal partitioning is suitable for managing large datasets across time or logical segments. By implementing vertical and horizontal partitioning, you enhanced the organization and performance of the AdventureWorks database, providing flexible strategies for managing large tables effectively.

Recipe #3: Perform Attaching, Detaching, and Dropping Partitions

Partitions can be dynamically managed by attaching, detaching, and dropping them as needed. This flexibility allows for effective data management over time. This recipe will instruct the processes of attaching new partitions, detaching existing ones, and safely dropping partitions from the database.

Attach a New Partition

Attaching partitions involves adding new data segments to a partitioned table. Detaching partitions allows you to remove data segments without dropping them immediately, and dropping partitions completely removes them from the database.

These operations help in managing data lifecycle, such as archiving old data or adding new data segments. Suppose you need to add a new partition for orders placed in February 2024:

```
CREATE TABLE orders_202402 (

  order_date DATE NOT NULL,

  customer_id INTEGER NOT NULL,

  total_due NUMERIC(12, 2)

)

PARTITION OF orders

FOR VALUES FROM ('2024-02-01') TO ('2024-03-01');
```

Use the **ALTER TABLE** command to attach the new partition:

```
ALTER TABLE orders

ATTACH PARTITION orders_202402

FOR VALUES FROM ('2024-02-01') TO ('2024-03-01');
```

This step incorporates the new partition into the existing **orders** table.

Detach an Existing Partition

Detaching a partition allows you to remove it from the parent table without deleting the data immediately. This can be useful for archiving:

```
ALTER TABLE orders

DETACH PARTITION orders_202302;
```

After detachment, **orders_202302** becomes an independent table but retains its data.

Drop a Detached Partition

Once detached, partitions can be safely dropped if the data is no longer needed:

```
DROP TABLE orders_202302;
```

Dropping a table permanently deletes the data, so ensure it is backed up if necessary. Use PostgreSQL system views to verify partition management operations:

```
SELECT partition_name, partition_bound

FROM information_schema.partitions

WHERE table_name = 'orders';
```

By dynamically managing partitions through attaching, detaching, and dropping, you ensured flexible and efficient data management for the database, optimizing for both current and future needs.

Recipe #4: Tables Partitioning using Table Inheritance

Table inheritance allows for the creation of partitioned tables by inheriting the structure of a parent table. This approach is flexible and allows for adding specific constraints or indexes to child tables. In this recipe, you'll learn how to use table inheritance for partitioning the database.

Create Child Tables using Inheritance

The parent table defines the overall structure that child tables will inherit. For the **orders** table in the database, you can define a parent table:

```
CREATE TABLE orders_parent (
  id SERIAL PRIMARY KEY,
  order_date DATE NOT NULL,
  customer_id INTEGER NOT NULL,
  total_due NUMERIC(12, 2)
);
```

Create child tables for each partition using the **INHERITS** clause:

```
CREATE TABLE orders_202301 (
  CHECK (order_date >= '2023-01-01' AND order_date <
'2023-02-01')
) INHERITS (orders_parent);
CREATE TABLE orders_202302 (
  CHECK (order_date >= '2023-02-01' AND order_date <
'2023-03-01')
) INHERITS (orders_parent);
```

Each child table inherits the structure of **orders_parent** and includes a check constraint to define its partition range.

Create Indexes on Child Tables

Insert data into the parent table, and PostgreSQL will automatically route the data to the appropriate child table based on the constraints:

```
INSERT INTO orders_parent (order_date, customer_id,
total_due)

VALUES ('2023-01-15', 789, 200.00);
```

Query the parent table, and PostgreSQL will handle routing to child tables:

```
SELECT * FROM orders_parent WHERE order_date BETWEEN
'2023-01-01' AND '2023-02-01';
```

Indexes can be created on child tables for optimized query performance:

```
CREATE INDEX idx_orders_202301_customer_id ON
orders_202301 (customer_id);
```

Monitor and Adjust Partition Strategy

Use **VACUUM** and **ANALYZE** to maintain table performance:

```
VACUUM ANALYZE orders_202301;
```

Use system views to monitor table performance and adjust strategies as needed:

```
SELECT table_name, reltuples, relpages

FROM pg_class

WHERE relname LIKE 'orders_%';
```

Table inheritance provides flexibility in partition management, especially when constraints or additional attributes need to be applied to specific partitions. By using table inheritance for partitioning, you implemented a flexible strategy for managing large tables in the database, allowing for specialized configurations and optimizations for each partition.

Recipe #5: Implement Automatic Partitioning

Automatic partitioning simplifies the management of large tables by automatically creating and managing partitions based on predefined rules. This recipe will demonstrate how to implement automatic partitioning for the AdventureWorks database.

Create Initial Partitions

Use the **PARTITION BY** clause to define a table that automatically handles partition creation based on specified criteria:

```
CREATE TABLE orders (

  id SERIAL PRIMARY KEY,

  order_date DATE NOT NULL,

  customer_id INTEGER NOT NULL,

  total_due NUMERIC(12, 2)

)

PARTITION BY RANGE (order_date);
```

Define initial partitions to handle data based on expected patterns:

```
CREATE TABLE orders_2023 PARTITION OF orders

FOR VALUES FROM ('2023-01-01') TO ('2024-01-01');
```

Implement Automatic Partition Creation

Create a function to automate partition creation:

```
CREATE OR REPLACE FUNCTION create_monthly_partition()
```

```
RETURNS void AS $$
DECLARE
  partition_name TEXT;
  start_date DATE;
  end_date DATE;
BEGIN
  start_date := date_trunc('month', CURRENT_DATE) + INTERVAL '1 month';
  end_date := start_date + INTERVAL '1 month';
  partition_name := 'orders_' || to_char(start_date, 'YYYYMM');

  EXECUTE format('CREATE TABLE %I PARTITION OF orders FOR VALUES FROM (%L) TO (%L)',
                 partition_name, start_date, end_date);
END;
$$ LANGUAGE plpgsql;
```

Schedule this function to run monthly using **pg_cron** or another scheduling tool:

```
SELECT cron.schedule('0 0 1 * *', 'SELECT create_monthly_partition();');
```

Test Automatic Partitioning

Insert data and verify that it is automatically routed to the appropriate partition:

```
INSERT INTO orders (order_date, customer_id, total_due)

VALUES ('2024-01-15', 1010, 250.00);
```

Use system views to ensure new partitions are created and data is correctly partitioned:

```
SELECT partition_name, partition_bound

FROM information_schema.partitions

WHERE table_name = 'orders';
```

Perform tests to verify that automatic partitioning behaves as expected. Ensure that queries leverage partition pruning for efficiency:

```
SELECT * FROM orders WHERE order_date BETWEEN '2024-01-
01' AND '2024-01-31';
```

Ensure that queries leverage partition pruning for optimal efficiency, checking that only relevant partitions are scanned during query execution. As the AdventureWorks database continues to grow, evaluate your partitioning strategy periodically to ensure it aligns with your data and query patterns. Consider adjusting partition sizes or ranges as needed to maintain performance and manageability.

By implementing automatic partitioning, you streamlined the management of large tables in the database, reducing manual intervention and ensuring efficient data organization. This approach helps maintain performance and scalability, allowing you to focus on other critical aspects of database management.

Recipe #6: Run Declarative Partitioning

Declarative partitioning allows for a more streamlined and efficient way of managing large datasets by automatically distributing data across partitions based on predefined criteria. This approach leverages the power of partitioning to enhance query performance and simplify data management. In this recipe, you will learn how to implement declarative partitioning in the database.

Understand Declarative Partitioning:

Declarative partitioning allows you to define partitions using simple SQL statements. It simplifies the process of partition management and is supported in PostgreSQL versions 10 and later. This method provides flexibility and ease of use compared to older partitioning methods like inheritance, making it suitable for modern data management needs.

Use the **PARTITION BY** clause to define a partitioned table. For the database, we will partition the **orders** table by month using the **order_date** column:

```
CREATE TABLE orders (
  id SERIAL PRIMARY KEY,
  order_date DATE NOT NULL,
  customer_id INTEGER NOT NULL,
  total_due NUMERIC(12, 2)
)
PARTITION BY RANGE (order_date);
```

This command creates a partitioned **orders** table, specifying **order_date** as the partition key and using range partitioning.

Automate Partition Creation

Define partitions for each month to handle data distribution effectively:

```
CREATE TABLE orders_202301 PARTITION OF orders
FOR VALUES FROM ('2023-01-01') TO ('2023-02-01');
CREATE TABLE orders_202302 PARTITION OF orders
FOR VALUES FROM ('2023-02-01') TO ('2023-03-01');
CREATE TABLE orders_202303 PARTITION OF orders
FOR VALUES FROM ('2023-03-01') TO ('2023-04-01');
```

Each partition corresponds to a specific date range, allowing data to be neatly organized by month.

Implement a procedure to automate the creation of new partitions as data grows, leveraging a function and scheduling mechanism:

```
CREATE OR REPLACE FUNCTION create_monthly_partition()

RETURNS void AS $$

DECLARE

  partition_name TEXT;

  start_date DATE;

  end_date DATE;

BEGIN

  start_date := date_trunc('month', CURRENT_DATE) +
INTERVAL '1 month';

  end_date := start_date + INTERVAL '1 month';

  partition_name := 'orders_' || to_char(start_date,
'YYYYMM');


  EXECUTE format('CREATE TABLE %I PARTITION OF orders FOR
VALUES FROM (%L) TO (%L)',

                 partition_name, start_date, end_date);

END;

$$ LANGUAGE plpgsql;
```

Query Partitioned Data

Use **pg_cron** or a similar scheduling tool to automate the execution of the partition creation function:

```
SELECT cron.schedule('0 0 1 * *', 'SELECT
create_monthly_partition();');
```

This setup ensures that new partitions are created automatically at the start of each month. Insert data as usual, and PostgreSQL will automatically route the data to the appropriate partition based on the **order_date**:

```
INSERT INTO orders (order_date, customer_id, total_due)

VALUES ('2023-04-15', 234, 350.00);
```

Query the partitioned table, leveraging partition pruning to improve query performance by scanning only relevant partitions:

```
SELECT * FROM orders WHERE order_date BETWEEN '2023-02-
01' AND '2023-02-28';
```

Use system views to monitor partition health and performance, performing maintenance tasks like **VACUUM** and **ANALYZE** as needed:

```
SELECT partition_name, partition_bound FROM
information_schema.partitions WHERE table_name =
'orders';
```

By implementing declarative partitioning, you streamlined data management and enhanced query performance for the database, leveraging PostgreSQL's powerful partitioning features.

Recipe #7: Configure Sharding with FWD and CitusData

Sharding is a technique used to horizontally scale databases by distributing data across multiple nodes. You can use Flexible Web Data (FWD) and CitusData to implement sharding, allowing you to handle larger datasets and improve performance. This combined recipe will instruct setting up sharding for the AdventureWorks database.

Setup FWD

Sharding involves splitting a database into smaller, more manageable pieces called shards, which are stored on separate database instances or nodes. Each shard contains a subset of the data, allowing for parallel processing and improved performance. FWD and CitusData are popular tools for implementing sharding in PostgreSQL, each offering unique features and benefits.

Select a column to use as the sharding key, which determines how data is distributed across shards. For the AdventureWorks database, the **customer_id** column is a suitable choice, as it evenly distributes data and aligns with common query patterns. To begin, create a shard map table to map **customer_id** values to specific shards:

```
CREATE TABLE shard_map (

  customer_id INTEGER PRIMARY KEY,

  shard_id INTEGER

);
```

Populate the shard map with data, assigning each **customer_id** to a specific shard:

```
INSERT INTO shard_map (customer_id, shard_id) VALUES (1,
1), (2, 2), (3, 1), (4, 2);
```

Configure FWD to route queries to the appropriate shard based on the shard map. This typically involves setting up a middleware layer to intercept queries and direct them to the correct node.

Configure Sharding with CitusData

Install the Citus extension on each node where you want to store data:

```
CREATE EXTENSION citus;
```

Use the **CREATE TABLE** statement with the **DISTRIBUTED BY** clause to create a distributed table based on the **customer_id** column:

```
CREATE TABLE orders (

  id SERIAL PRIMARY KEY,
```

```
  order_date DATE NOT NULL,
  customer_id INTEGER NOT NULL,
  total_due NUMERIC(12, 2)
) DISTRIBUTED BY (customer_id);
```

Add additional nodes to the Citus cluster using the **citus_add_node** command:

```
SELECT master_add_node('node1.gitforgits.com', 5432);
SELECT master_add_node('node2.gitforgits.com', 5432);
```

Use tools like **pg_dump** and **pg_restore** or custom scripts to migrate data from the original table to the distributed or sharded table. Ensure data is correctly placed in the appropriate shards based on the sharding key. Then, execute queries on the sharded table, leveraging the distributed architecture for improved performance:

```
SELECT * FROM orders WHERE customer_id = 2;
```

Implement strategies like indexing and query optimization to enhance performance:

```
SELECT shardid, count(*) FROM orders WHERE total_due >
500 GROUP BY shardid;
```

By configuring sharding with FWD and CitusData, you scaled the AdventureWorks database horizontally, enhancing its ability to handle large datasets and improving overall performance. This setup allows for efficient data distribution and query processing across multiple nodes.

Summary

To sum up, you learned all about advanced partitioning and sharding strategies in PostgreSQL. You explored declarative partitioning, which simplifies data management by automatically distributing data across partitions based on predefined criteria, thereby enhancing query performance. The chapter covered how to dynamically manage partitions by attaching, detaching, and dropping them, providing flexibility to handle data growth and archiving requirements effectively. Additionally, you discovered how to implement sharding using tools like FWD and

CitusData to distribute data across multiple nodes.

This approach enabled you to scale the AdventureWorks database horizontally, improving its capacity to handle larger datasets and boosting overall performance. Sharding allowed for better load balancing across shards, enhancing query processing capabilities and ensuring high availability. Overall, this chapter equipped you with in-depth knowledge of partitioning and sharding techniques, empowering you to manage large datasets effectively and optimize your databases for performance and scalability in diverse environments.

CHAPTER 7: TROUBLESHOOTING REPLICATION, SCALABILITY & HIGH AVAILABILITY

Introduction

Here you will learn all about PostgreSQL's advanced features, including replication, scalability, and high availability. In this chapter, you will learn the ins and outs of master-slave replication, a technique that lets you build replica databases with read queries and data redundancy built right in. To keep your database data consistent and available across all of your nodes, you'll configure the master and slave nodes, set up replication slots, and monitor the replication process.

Additionally, you will explore the setup and administration of repmgr, a powerful tool for PostgreSQL replication cluster management. You will learn the ins and outs of database cloning, node registration, and failover process management to guarantee high availability and reduce downtime in the event of failures. Additionally, you will be concentrating on utilizing Patroni, a tool that streamlines PostgreSQL cluster management by automating replication and failover procedures, to deploy high-availability clusters. To guarantee smooth transitions between primary and standby nodes, you will need to configure Patroni on each node, set up a distributed configuration store like etcd, and test failover scenarios.

Lastly, you will learn how to upgrade databases on a replication cluster so that updates to the newest version can be made to both primary and standby instances without causing service interruptions. Among these tasks is the execution of upgrade scripts, the checking of replication status, and the testing of the enhanced environment's compatibility and performance.

Recipe #1: Using Master-Slave Replication

Master-Slave replication is a powerful technique that helps ensure high availability and scalability by creating a replica (slave) of the master database. This replica can handle read queries, reducing the load on the master database and providing redundancy in case of failure. In this recipe, you will learn how to set up and manage master-slave replication using streaming replication.

Create Replication

Ensure that PostgreSQL 16 is installed on your master server. Use the following command to install it:

```
sudo apt-get update

sudo apt-get install postgresql-16
```

Edit the **postgresql.conf** file to enable replication:

```
wal_level = replica
```

```
max_wal_senders = 10

wal_keep_size = 64  # MB, ensure WAL files are retained
long enough
```

Open the **pg_hba.conf** file to allow connections from slave servers:

```
host replication replication_user <SLAVE_IP_ADDRESS>/32
md5
```

Restart PostgreSQL to apply the changes:

```
sudo systemctl restart postgresql
```

Connect to the PostgreSQL database and create a user with replication privileges:

```
CREATE USER replication_user WITH REPLICATION ENCRYPTED
PASSWORD 'password';
```

Replication slots help manage WAL retention and ensure the slave can reconnect if there are interruptions:

```
SELECT * FROM
pg_create_physical_replication_slot('replication_slot');
```

Setup Slave Database and Monitor Replication

Install PostgreSQL 16 on the slave server similarly to the master setup. Stop the PostgreSQL service if it is running:

```
sudo systemctl stop postgresql
```

Use **pg_basebackup** to copy the master database to the slave server:

```
pg_basebackup -h <MASTER_IP_ADDRESS> -D
/var/lib/postgresql/16/main -U replication_user -P --
slot=replication_slot --write-recovery-conf
```

This command creates a base backup of the master and sets up the recovery configuration for the slave. Edit the **postgresql.conf** file on the slave to enable hot standby:

```
hot_standby = on
```

Ensure that **standby.signal** file exists in the data directory to designate this as a standby server.

Start the PostgreSQL service on the slave server:

```
sudo systemctl start postgresql
```

Verify replication by checking the status on the slave server:

```
SELECT * FROM pg_stat_wal_receiver;
```

Use system views on the master to monitor replication status and performance:

```
SELECT client_addr, state, sent_lsn, write_lsn,
flush_lsn, replay_lsn FROM pg_stat_replication;
```

Repeat the steps for setting up additional slave databases to further distribute read load and increase redundancy. By setting up master-slave replication, you ensured high availability and scalability for the database, allowing for efficient load distribution and redundancy.

Recipe #2: Install and Configure 'repmgr'

repmgr is a powerful tool for managing PostgreSQL replication clusters, offering automated failover, monitoring, and management capabilities. This recipe will demonstrate installing and configuring **repmgr** to enhance replication management in your PostgreSQL environment.

Getting Started with 'repmgr'

Install **repmgr** on all nodes in the replication cluster:

```
sudo apt-get update

sudo apt-get install postgresql-16-repmgr
```

Ensure that PostgreSQL client packages are installed on all nodes:

```
sudo apt-get install postgresql-client-16
```

On each node, create a **repmgr** user with necessary privileges:

```
CREATE USER repmgr WITH SUPERUSER LOGIN ENCRYPTED
PASSWORD 'password';
```

Create a **repmgr** database on each node:

```
CREATE DATABASE repmgr WITH OWNER repmgr;
```

On the primary node, configure the **repmgr.conf** file with connection information and replication settings:

```
node_id = 1

node_name = 'primary'

conninfo = 'host=primary_ip_address dbname=repmgr
user=repmgr password=password'

data_directory = '/var/lib/postgresql/16/main'
```

Ensure the file is copied to each standby node with appropriate modifications for each node.

Managing Nodes

On the primary node, register it with **repmgr**:

```
sudo -u postgres repmgr -f /etc/repmgr.conf primary
register
```

Check the cluster setup to ensure the primary node is correctly registered:

```
sudo -u postgres repmgr -f /etc/repmgr.conf cluster show
```

Use **repmgr** to clone the primary node on each standby node:

```
sudo -u postgres repmgr -f /etc/repmgr.conf standby clone
primary_ip_address
```

Register each standby node with **repmgr**:

```
sudo -u postgres repmgr -f /etc/repmgr.conf standby
register
```

Monitor and Manage Replication

Use **repmgr** to monitor the cluster and verify that all nodes are synchronized:

```
sudo -u postgres repmgr -f /etc/repmgr.conf cluster show
```

In the event of a failure, use **repmgr** to promote a standby node:

```
sudo -u postgres repmgr -f /etc/repmgr.conf standby
promote
```

repmgr offers features like automatic failover, reconfiguration, and monitoring. By installing and configuring **repmgr**, you enhanced the management and monitoring of your PostgreSQL replication cluster, ensuring robust failover capabilities and streamlined operations.

Recipe #3: Cloning Database with 'repmgr'

Cloning a PostgreSQL database using **repmgr** is an efficient way to create new standby nodes by copying existing primary or standby nodes. This recipe will instruct the process of cloning databases within a replication cluster using **repmgr**.

Configure 'repmgr.conf'

Decide which node in the replication cluster will serve as the source for cloning. This can be either a primary node or an existing standby node, depending on your needs. On the new node, configure the **repmgr.conf** file with connection details and replication settings similar to other nodes:

```
node_id = <NEW_NODE_ID>

node_name = 'standby_new'

conninfo = 'host=new_ip_address dbname=repmgr user=repmgr
password=password'

data_directory = '/var/lib/postgresql/16/main'
```

Clone the Source Node

Execute the **repmgr standby clone** command to clone the source node to the new node:

```
sudo -u postgres repmgr -h source_ip_address -f
/etc/repmgr.conf standby clone
```

Confirm that the cloning process was successful by checking the replication status on the new node:

```
sudo -u postgres repmgr -f /etc/repmgr.conf cluster show
```

Register the new standby node with the cluster using **repmgr**:

```
sudo -u postgres repmgr -f /etc/repmgr.conf standby
register
```

Verify that the new node is registered and functioning as a standby by checking the cluster status:

```
sudo -u postgres repmgr -f /etc/repmgr.conf cluster show
```

Streaming Replication

Verify that streaming replication is functioning correctly between the new standby node and the source node:

```
SELECT * FROM pg_stat_replication;
```

Keep an eye on replication lag to ensure the new node remains up-to-date with changes from the primary node:

```
SELECT client_addr, state, sent_lsn, write_lsn,
flush_lsn, replay_lsn FROM pg_stat_replication;
```

Test failover procedures to ensure the new standby node can take over if necessary:

```
sudo -u postgres repmgr -f /etc/repmgr.conf standby
promote
```

Confirm the new node's promotion by checking the replication status and ensuring it is now acting as the primary node:

```
sudo -u postgres repmgr -f /etc/repmgr.conf cluster show
```

By following these steps, you effectively cloned a PostgreSQL database using **repmgr**, adding a new standby node to the replication cluster.

Recipe #4: Deploy High Availability Cluster with Patroni

Patroni is an open-source tool that provides high availability for PostgreSQL by managing failover and replication within a cluster. It leverages a distributed configuration store like etcd, Consul, or ZooKeeper to coordinate the cluster state. This recipe will demonstrate setting up a high-availability PostgreSQL cluster using Patroni and etcd.

Up and Running with 'etcd'

Install etcd on a separate server to store the cluster configuration and state information. Use the following command to install etcd:

```
sudo apt-get update

sudo apt-get install etcd
```

Edit the etcd configuration file to set the listening address and advertise the client URL:

```
ETCD_LISTEN_CLIENT_URLS="http://0.0.0.0:2379"

ETCD_ADVERTISE_CLIENT_URLS="http://<etcd_ip_address>:2379
"
```

Start the etcd service and verify that it is running:

```
sudo systemctl start etcd

sudo systemctl enable etcd

etcdctl cluster-health
```

Configuring Patroni

Install Patroni on each node in the PostgreSQL cluster:

```
sudo apt-get install python3-pip

sudo pip3 install patroni
```

Create a Patroni configuration file (**patroni.yml**) for each node with the following settings:

```
scope: postgres-cluster

namespace: /service/

name: node1

restapi:

  listen: 0.0.0.0:8008

  connect_address: <node1_ip_address>:8008


etcd:
```

```
  host: <etcd_ip_address>:2379

bootstrap:
  dcs:
    ttl: 30
    loop_wait: 10
    retry_timeout: 10
    maximum_lag_on_failover: 1048576
    postgresql:
      use_pg_rewind: true
      parameters:
        wal_level: replica
        hot_standby: "on"
        wal_keep_size: 64
        max_wal_senders: 5
        max_replication_slots: 5

  initdb:
  - encoding: UTF8
  - locale: en_US.UTF-8
```

```yaml
postgresql:
  listen: 0.0.0.0:5432
  connect_address: <node1_ip_address>:5432
  data_dir: /var/lib/postgresql/16/main
  bin_dir: /usr/lib/postgresql/16/bin
  authentication:
    superuser:
      username: postgres
      password: mypassword
    replication:
      username: replicator
      password: mypassword

tags:
  nofailover: false
  noloadbalance: false
  clonefrom: false
  nosync: false
```

Replace **<node1_ip_address>** and **<etcd_ip_address>** with actual IP addresses for each node and etcd server.

Verify Replication

On the primary node, start Patroni using the following command:

```
sudo patroni /etc/patroni.yml
```

Ensure that the cluster forms correctly and that the primary node is elected. Check the Patroni logs and use the REST API to query the cluster state:

```
curl http://<node1_ip_address>:8008/cluster
```

On each standby node, start Patroni with the appropriate configuration file:

```
sudo patroni /etc/patroni.yml
```

Use Patroni's REST API or logs to ensure that replication is functioning correctly and that standby nodes are synchronizing with the primary node:

```
curl http://<node2_ip_address>:8008/cluster
```

Test Failover

Stop the PostgreSQL service on the primary node to simulate a failure:

```
sudo systemctl stop postgresql
```

Patroni should automatically promote one of the standby nodes to become the new primary. Verify the failover by querying the cluster state:

```
curl http://<node2_ip_address>:8008/cluster
```

Patroni provides various features such as monitoring, logging, and integration with other tools. By deploying a high-availability cluster with Patroni, you ensured robust failover capabilities and automated replication management for the database, enhancing its resilience and performance.

Recipe #5: Using HAProxy and PgBouncer for High Availability

HAProxy and PgBouncer are open-source tools used to improve PostgreSQL's high availability and scalability by providing load balancing and connection pooling. This recipe will demonstrate setting up HAProxy and PgBouncer for your PostgreSQL cluster.

Start HAProxy

Install HAProxy on a separate server that will act as the load balancer:

```
sudo apt-get update

sudo apt-get install haproxy
```

Edit the HAProxy configuration file (**/etc/haproxy/haproxy.cfg**) to define the frontend and backend settings:

```
frontend pg_front

  bind *:5432

  mode tcp

  default_backend pg_back


backend pg_back

  mode tcp

  option pgsql-check

  balance roundrobin

  server node1 <node1_ip_address>:5432 check

  server node2 <node2_ip_address>:5432 check

  server node3 <node3_ip_address>:5432 check
```

Replace **<node1_ip_address>**, **<node2_ip_address>**, and **<node3_ip_address>** with the IP addresses of your PostgreSQL nodes.

Restart the HAProxy service to apply the changes:

```
sudo systemctl restart haproxy
```

Configuring PgBouncer

Install PgBouncer on the same server as HAProxy or on each PostgreSQL node to manage connection pooling:

```
sudo apt-get install pgbouncer
```

Edit the PgBouncer configuration file (**/etc/pgbouncer/pgbouncer.ini**) with the following settings:

```
[databases]

adventureworks = host=localhost port=5432
dbname=adventureworks


[pgbouncer]

listen_addr = *

listen_port = 6432

auth_type = md5

auth_file = /etc/pgbouncer/userlist.txt

pool_mode = session

max_client_conn = 100

default_pool_size = 20
```

Create a **userlist.txt** file to store user credentials:

```
"postgres" "md5<hashed_password>"
```

Start the PgBouncer service:

```
sudo systemctl start pgbouncer
```

Monitor HAProxy and PgBouncer

Ensure that PostgreSQL nodes are configured to accept connections from the HAProxy and PgBouncer servers. Update the **pg_hba.conf** file on each node:

```
host all all <haproxy_ip_address>/32 md5

host all all <pgbouncer_ip_address>/32 md5
```

Connect to PostgreSQL through HAProxy and verify that connections are being distributed across nodes:

```
psql -h <haproxy_ip_address> -p 5432 -U postgres -d
adventureworks
```

Use PgBouncer to manage connections and verify that pooling is functioning correctly:

```
psql -h <pgbouncer_ip_address> -p 6432 -U postgres -d
adventureworks
```

Enable statistics in **haproxy.cfg** if not already enabled:

```
listen stats

  bind :8404

  stats enable

  stats uri /

  stats refresh 10s
```

Simulate a failure of one of the PostgreSQL nodes by stopping its service:

```
sudo systemctl stop postgresql
```

Check that HAProxy redirects traffic to the remaining nodes and that PgBouncer continues to pool connections seamlessly. Use the HAProxy stats page to see which nodes are active and handling requests.

HAProxy and PgBouncer can be integrated with orchestration tools like Kubernetes or Docker for enhanced scalability and management. By setting up HAProxy and PgBouncer, you achieved high availability and improved performance for your PostgreSQL cluster, allowing for efficient load balancing and connection pooling across multiple nodes.

Recipe #6: Perform Database Upgrade on Replication Cluster

Upgrading a PostgreSQL replication cluster involves updating both primary and standby instances to a new version, ensuring compatibility and minimizing downtime. This recipe will demonstrate upgrading a PostgreSQL cluster while maintaining replication and high availability.

Run the Upgrade Script

Perform a full backup of your primary and standby databases to ensure data safety in case of any issues during the upgrade process:

```
pg_dumpall -h <primary_ip_address> -U postgres >
full_backup.sql
```

Review PostgreSQL's release notes for changes and compatibility considerations between versions. On the primary database instance, stop the PostgreSQL service:

```
sudo systemctl stop postgresql
```

Install the new version of PostgreSQL on the primary instance:

```
sudo apt-get install postgresql-17
```

Use **pg_upgrade** to upgrade the data directory to the new version:

```
pg_upgrade -b /usr/lib/postgresql/16/bin -B
/usr/lib/postgresql/17/bin -d /var/lib/postgresql/16/main
-D /var/lib/postgresql/17/main -U postgres
```

Review and update configuration files (**postgresql.conf** and **pg_hba.conf**) for compatibility with the new version. Then, start the PostgreSQL service on the primary instance:

```
sudo systemctl start postgresql
```

Verify that the primary database is functioning correctly by checking logs and running basic queries.

Then, on each standby database instance, stop the PostgreSQL service:

```
sudo systemctl stop postgresql
```

Install the new version of PostgreSQL on each standby instance:

```
sudo apt-get install postgresql-17
```

Use **pg_upgrade** to upgrade the data directory on each standby:

```
pg_upgrade -b /usr/lib/postgresql/16/bin -B
/usr/lib/postgresql/17/bin -d /var/lib/postgresql/16/main
-D /var/lib/postgresql/17/main -U postgres
```

Test the Upgrade

Ensure that configuration files are consistent with the primary instance and compatible with the new version. Start the PostgreSQL service on each standby instance:

```
sudo systemctl start postgresql
```

Verify that replication is functioning correctly by checking the replication status on each standby node:

```
SELECT * FROM pg_stat_replication;
```

Ensure that all standby nodes are fully synchronized with the primary instance by checking logs and system views. In case of issues, plan a rollback strategy using the backups created before the upgrade.

By following these steps, you successfully upgraded the PostgreSQL replication cluster while maintaining high availability and ensuring minimal disruption to services. This approach allows you to take advantage of new features and improvements in the latest PostgreSQL version.

Recipe #7: Optimizing JSON Queries with SIMD Acceleration

We shall assume that the AdventureWorks database is experiencing performance bottlenecks with its analytical queries, particularly those involving JSON data processing. Users have reported slow query response times when analyzing this data, impacting business operations. The goal is to optimize these queries using PostgreSQL 16's SIMD acceleration to improve performance and efficiency.

In this recipe, we will see how to leverage SIMD acceleration in order to optimize JSON processing to improvise the query performance and reduce the execution times as well.

Analyze Performance Bottleneck

Begin by identifying the queries that are causing performance issues. For the **orders** table, a common analytical query might look like this:

```
SELECT order_id, jsonb_array_elements_text(order_details
-> 'items') AS item

FROM orders

WHERE (order_details ->> 'status') = 'completed';
```

Use **EXPLAIN ANALYZE** to assess the query execution plan and identify areas where performance improvements are possible:

```
EXPLAIN ANALYZE

SELECT order_id, jsonb_array_elements_text(order_details
-> 'items') AS item

FROM orders

WHERE (order_details ->> 'status') = 'completed';
```

Optimize the Query for SIMD

Restructure the query to take full advantage of SIMD acceleration. PostgreSQL 16 automatically uses SIMD where applicable, so focus on reducing any unnecessary computations and ensuring the query is well-optimized:

```
SELECT order_id, item

FROM (

  SELECT order_id,
jsonb_array_elements_text(order_details -> 'items') AS
item

  FROM orders

  WHERE (order_details ->> 'status') = 'completed'

) AS items_processed

WHERE item IS NOT NULL;
```

This subquery approach can help streamline data processing and make it more conducive to SIMD optimization by narrowing down the dataset earlier in the query plan. Then, execute the optimized query and compare the performance metrics against the original query using **EXPLAIN ANALYZE**:

```
EXPLAIN ANALYZE

SELECT order_id, item

FROM (

  SELECT order_id,
jsonb_array_elements_text(order_details -> 'items') AS
item

  FROM orders

  WHERE (order_details ->> 'status') = 'completed'
```

```
) AS items_processed
WHERE item IS NOT NULL;
```

Assess the overall performance improvements gained through SIMD acceleration. This should include faster query response times, reduced CPU usage, and improved throughput for analytical workloads. This entire approach is particularly valuable for data-intensive applications where query speed and resource efficiency are critical.

Summary

In this chapter, you learned about advanced replication, scalability, and high-availability techniques in PostgreSQL. You explored master-slave replication, which involved setting up replica databases to handle read queries and ensure data redundancy. This process included configuring replication slots and monitoring replication status to maintain data consistency and availability across the database environment. Additionally, you discovered how to install and configure repmgr to automate failover and manage PostgreSQL replication clusters, allowing for efficient database management and reduced downtime in case of failures.

The chapter also covered deploying high-availability clusters using Patroni, simplifying the management of PostgreSQL clusters by automating replication and failover processes. You learned how to set up a distributed configuration store, configure Patroni on each node, and test failover scenarios to ensure seamless transitions between primary and standby nodes. Finally, the chapter taught you through performing database upgrades on replication clusters, ensuring both primary and standby instances were updated without disrupting services, and also implementing SIMD acceleration to significantly enhance the performance of JSON queries.

CHAPTER 8: BLOB, JSON QUERY, CAST OPERATOR & CONNECTIONS

Introduction

In this chapter, you will be exploring the concepts of working with advanced data types and automation techniques in PostgreSQL. You will be learning how to import BLOB (Binary Large Object) data types using the **bytea** data type, allowing you to store and retrieve binary files such as images and audio. This will involve using a Python script to convert binary files into hex-encoded strings and inserting them into PostgreSQL tables. By understanding how to handle BLOB data, you will be able to manage complex data requirements within your database.

You will be discovering how to automate SQL query execution using shell scripts. This technique will enable you to streamline database operations and integrate PostgreSQL queries into larger workflows. You will create shell scripts that connect to the database, execute SQL commands, and handle connection details securely. By mastering shell scripting, you will enhance your ability to automate repetitive tasks and manage your PostgreSQL database efficiently. Furthermore, you will be focusing on working with JSON data in PostgreSQL, leveraging the JSON and JSONB data types to store and query semi-structured data. You will be practicing how to insert, query, update, and filter JSON data using PostgreSQL's powerful JSON functions and operators. By learning to manage JSON data, you will gain the flexibility to handle dynamic data structures and perform complex queries.

Finally, you will be exploring the use of the CAST operator to convert data types within PostgreSQL. This will include transforming data types in queries, inserts, updates, and filters, ensuring compatibility and accuracy across your database operations.

Recipe #1: Import BLOB Data Types

Binary Large Objects (BLOBs) are used in databases to store large binary files, such as images, audio, and other media. The **bytea** data type is used to store binary data. This recipe will teach you through importing BLOB data into a PostgreSQL table using a practical example.

Convert Binary File to Hex-Encoded String

Start by creating a new table with a **bytea** column to store BLOB data. Given below is an example of creating a table to store files:

```
CREATE TABLE files (
  id SERIAL PRIMARY KEY,
  file_name VARCHAR(255),
  file_data BYTEA
```

```
);
```

This command creates a table named **files** with columns for the file ID, file name, and binary data. Now before importing binary files into PostgreSQL, you must convert them to a hex-encoded string. You can use a Python script to achieve this conversion:

```
def convert_to_hex(file_path):
    with open(file_path, 'rb') as file:
        return '\\x' + file.read().hex()


file_path = 'path/to/your/file.ext'
hex_string = convert_to_hex(file_path)
print(hex_string)
```

Replace **'path/to/your/file.ext'** with the path to your binary file. This script reads the file and outputs its hex-encoded string representation.

Convert BLOB Data Back to Binary

With the hex-encoded string, you can now insert the BLOB data into your PostgreSQL table:

```
INSERT INTO files (file_name, file_data)
VALUES ('your_file_name.ext', E'\\xYOUR_HEX_STRING');
```

Replace **'your_file_name.ext'** with the file's name and **\\xYOUR_HEX_STRING** with the hex-encoded string from the Python script. Note that the prefix **E'\\x'** is required to indicate the data is hex-encoded.

To retrieve BLOB data, use a **SELECT** query:

```
SELECT file_name, file_data FROM files WHERE id = 1;
```

This query retrieves the file name and binary data for the specified record. To work with the

BLOB data in your application, convert it back to its original form as needed.

If you need to convert the BLOB data back to its original binary form, you can use Python:

```
def convert_from_hex(hex_string, output_path):
    binary_data = bytes.fromhex(hex_string[2:])  # Skip the '\\x'
    with open(output_path, 'wb') as file:
        file.write(binary_data)

hex_string = '\\xYOUR_HEX_STRING'
output_path = 'path/to/output/file.ext'
convert_from_hex(hex_string, output_path)
```

This script writes the binary data back to a file at the specified **output_path**.

Importing BLOBs is useful for applications that require storage and retrieval of binary files. By following these steps, you imported BLOB data into a PostgreSQL table using the **bytea** data type, enabling the storage and retrieval of large binary objects in your database.

Recipe #2: Running Queries using Shell Script

Running SQL queries via shell scripts is an efficient way to automate database tasks and integrate PostgreSQL operations into broader workflows. This recipe will teach you through creating a shell script that connects to a PostgreSQL database and executes SQL commands.

Create Executable Shell Script

Start by creating a new shell script file with a **.sh** extension:

```
touch query_example.sh
```

Open the file in a text editor and add the following script:

```
#!/bin/bash

# Replace these variables with your PostgreSQL
credentials

DB_NAME="adventureworks"

DB_USER="your_postgresql_username"

DB_PASS="your_postgresql_password"

DB_HOST="localhost"

DB_PORT="5432"


# SQL query to execute

QUERY="SELECT * FROM product;"


# Execute the SQL query using psql

export PGPASSWORD="$DB_PASS"

psql -h "$DB_HOST" -p "$DB_PORT" -U "$DB_USER" -d
"$DB_NAME" -c "$QUERY"

unset PGPASSWORD
```

Replace placeholders with actual values for your PostgreSQL setup: **DB_NAME**, **DB_USER**, **DB_PASS**, and any other connection details like **DB_HOST** and **DB_PORT**.

Use the **chmod** command to make the shell script executable:

```
chmod +x query_example.sh
```

This step ensures you can run the script from the command line.

Execute the shell script to run the SQL query:

```
./query_example.sh
```

The script will connect to the specified PostgreSQL database and execute the given SQL query, displaying the results in the terminal.

Modify the **QUERY** variable in the shell script to execute different SQL queries. You can add more queries by creating new variables or appending additional **psql** commands. Ensure that SQL queries are enclosed in quotes and end with a semicolon.

Integrate Script into Automation Workflow

You can loop through multiple queries within the script using a **for** or **while** loop:

```
QUERIES=("SELECT * FROM product;" "SELECT * FROM
orders;")

for QUERY in "${QUERIES[@]}"

do

  psql -h "$DB_HOST" -p "$DB_PORT" -U "$DB_USER" -d
"$DB_NAME" -c "$QUERY"

done
```

Implement error handling to manage potential issues during query execution:

```
if ! psql -h "$DB_HOST" -p "$DB_PORT" -U "$DB_USER" -d
"$DB_NAME" -c "$QUERY"; then

  echo "Failed to execute query."

  exit 1

fi
```

Use cron jobs to schedule shell scripts for regular execution, automating routine database tasks. Create a cron job by editing the crontab file:

```
crontab -e
```

Add a new entry to schedule the script:

```
0 2 * * * /path/to/query_example.sh
```

By creating and running shell scripts, you automated PostgreSQL queries and integrated them into your broader data management workflows, streamlining operations and enhancing productivity.

Recipe #3: Working with PostgreSQL JSON Data

PostgreSQL offers robust support for JSON data through its JSON and JSONB data types, allowing you to store and query semi-structured data efficiently. This recipe will demonstrate how to work with JSON data using the database.

Create a Table with JSONB Data

Start by creating a table with a JSONB column to store JSON data. The given below example demonstrates storing customer information:

```
CREATE TABLE customer_info (

  id SERIAL PRIMARY KEY,

  data JSONB

);
```

The **customer_info** table has an **id** column for unique identifiers and a **data** column to store JSON data. Insert JSON data into the table, representing customer information:

```
INSERT INTO customer_info (data) VALUES

('{"name": "John Doe", "email": "john@gitforgits.com",
"age": 30, "address": {"street": "123 Main St", "city":
"New York", "state": "NY", "zip": "10001"}}'),
```

```
('{"name": "Jane Doe", "email": "jane@gitforgits.com",
"age": 28, "address": {"street": "456 Main St", "city":
"New York", "state": "NY", "zip": "10002"}}');
```

This command inserts two records into the **customer_info** table, each containing a JSON object with nested fields.

Query JSON Data:

Use PostgreSQL's JSON operators and functions to query JSON data efficiently. Extract specific fields from JSON data using the **->>** operator:

```
SELECT data->>'name' AS name FROM customer_info;
```

This query returns the **name** field from each JSON object as a separate column. Then, filter rows using JSON field values:

```
SELECT * FROM customer_info WHERE (data->>'age')::integer
>= 30;
```

This query returns all records where the **age** field is greater than or equal to 30. Modify JSON data within a table using the **jsonb_set** function:

```
UPDATE customer_info

SET data = jsonb_set(data, '{address,zip}', '"10003"')

WHERE data->>'email' = 'john@gitforgits.com';
```

This command updates the **zip** field in the **address** object for the record with the specified email. Use the **?** operator to check for the existence of specific fields within JSON data:

```
SELECT * FROM customer_info WHERE data ? 'email';
```

This query returns all records that contain the **email** field in their JSON data. Consider indexing JSONB columns using the **GIN** index for faster query performance, especially for frequently queried fields. By following these steps, you learned to store, query, and manipulate JSON data in PostgreSQL, providing powerful tools for managing semi-structured data within the database.

Recipe #4: Working with PostgreSQL CAST Operator

The CAST operator allows you to convert data from one type to another, providing flexibility in data manipulation and ensuring compatibility across operations. This recipe will show you how to use the CAST operator effectively in the database.

Convert Data Types

Use the CAST operator to change data types within queries. The below given example demonstrates converting a column to an integer:

```
SELECT CAST(total_due AS INTEGER) FROM orders;
```

Alternatively, you can use the `::` syntax for casting:

```
SELECT total_due::INTEGER FROM orders;
```

This converts the **total_due** column values from numeric to integer type. Convert data types during insertion to ensure compatibility with column definitions:

```
INSERT INTO prices (price) VALUES (CAST('10.50' AS
NUMERIC(10, 2)));
```

Using the `::` syntax:

```
INSERT INTO prices (price) VALUES ('10.50'::NUMERIC(10,
2));
```

These commands insert a string value as a numeric type into the **prices** table. Apply type conversions during updates to modify data accurately:

```
UPDATE prices SET price = CAST('15.75' AS NUMERIC(10, 2))
WHERE id = 1;
```

Using the `::` syntax:

```
UPDATE prices SET price = '15.75'::NUMERIC(10, 2) WHERE
id = 1;
```

These commands update the **price** column with a converted numeric value.

Filter Data

Convert data types within WHERE clauses to filter records effectively:

```
SELECT * FROM orders WHERE CAST(created_at AS DATE) =
'2023-10-01';
```

Using the **::** syntax:

```
SELECT * FROM orders WHERE created_at::DATE = '2023-10-
01';
```

These queries filter records based on a specific date by converting the **created_at** timestamp to a date type.

Leverage casting in complex queries and data transformations, using functions like **CAST()** and the **::** syntax to enhance data processing capabilities and ensure data integrity across your PostgreSQL database. By mastering the CAST operator, you gained the ability to transform and manipulate data types effectively within the database, enabling precise data handling and ensuring compatibility across diverse operations.

Summary

All in all, this chapter covered postgreSQL advanced data type management and process automation. You learned how to use the bytea data type to import BLOB data types, which lets you store binary files like audio and picture. This involved using a Python script to convert binary files into hex-encoded strings, which were then inserted into PostgreSQL tables. You also learned how to use shell scripts to automate the execution of SQL queries, which simplifies database operations by connecting to the database and safely running SQL commands.

Working with JSON data was also covered in this chapter, which taught you how to use JSON and JSONB data types to store and query semi-structured data. You gained knowledge of how to use the JSON functions and operators to insert, query, update, and filter JSON data. The chapter concluded with an explanation of how to convert data types in queries, inserts, updates, and filters using the CAST operator, which guarantees accuracy and compatibility across all database operations. All things considered, Chapter 8 taught useful techniques for working with various data kinds and automating PostgreSQL tasks.

CHAPTER 9: AUTHENTICATION, AUDIT & ENCRYPTION

Introduction

Learning PostgreSQL's more complex authentication and security features is the focus of this chapter. You will gain control over user access and permissions by learning how to manage roles, memberships, and authorizations. This include establishing roles and users, configuring role properties, and utilizing a variety of techniques for user authentication. You can improve the security of your PostgreSQL database and make sure that only authorized users can view and edit data by learning these techniques.

Additionally, you will learn how to configure SSL authentication to protect client-server connections in PostgreSQL. The steps involved in ensuring secure data transmission are creating SSL certificates, setting up PostgreSQL to use SSL, and testing the configuration. You will also be concentrating on using triggers and pgAudit to implement audit logging. By using these techniques, you'll be able to keep an eye on database activity and get a thorough audit trail of all database modifications. Installing and configuring pgAudit, making audit log tables, and putting triggers in place to record modifications to particular tables are all covered.

In the end, you will discover how to set up LDAP authentication, which enables PostgreSQL to perform user authentication against a centralized directory service. This method streamlines user management through the centralization of account control, the reduction of administrative burden, and the improvement of security. You can simplify user access across numerous apps and services by integrating LDAP authentication, assuring a safe and effective authentication procedure.

Recipe #1: Manage Roles, Membership Attributes, Authentication, and Authorizations

Roles are used to define users and groups, providing a flexible security model for managing access to the database. This recipe will teach you through creating roles, managing membership, and setting up authentication and authorization.

Manage Roles and Attributes

Roles in PostgreSQL can represent users, groups, or applications. Use the **CREATE ROLE** statement to define new roles:

```
CREATE ROLE sales;

CREATE ROLE marketing;
```

This command creates two roles: **sales** and **marketing**, which can be assigned specific permissions. Add users to roles using the **GRANT** statement to manage membership:

```
CREATE USER alice WITH PASSWORD 'alicepassword';

GRANT sales TO alice;
```

This command creates a user named **alice** and adds her to the **sales** role, granting her all permissions associated with that role. Next, define attributes such as login, password, and expiration using the **ALTER ROLE** statement:

```
ALTER ROLE sales LOGIN PASSWORD 'securepassword' VALID
UNTIL '2025-12-31';
```

This command sets a password and login attribute for the **sales** role, ensuring security and access control.

User Authentication

Specify authentication methods in the **pg_hba.conf** file. To use password authentication, configure the file with the **md5** method:

```
host    all             all             192.168.1.0/24
md5
```

Ensure you restart PostgreSQL to apply changes:

```
sudo systemctl restart postgresql
```

User Authorizations

Use the **GRANT** statement to assign specific permissions to users and roles:

```
GRANT SELECT, INSERT ON employees TO sales;
```

This command grants the **sales** role permission to select and insert records in the **employees** table. Revoke access when needed using the **REVOKE** statement:

```
REVOKE sales FROM alice;
```

This command removes **alice** from the **sales** role, revoking her permissions. Control access to database objects with **GRANT** and **REVOKE**:

```
GRANT SELECT ON products TO marketing;

REVOKE UPDATE ON products FROM marketing;
```

These commands grant the **marketing** role read access to the **products** table and revoke update permissions. By following these steps, you managed roles, memberships, authentication, and authorizations in PostgreSQL.

Recipe #2: Setting up SSL Authentication

SSL (Secure Sockets Layer) is used to encrypt connections between clients and PostgreSQL servers, enhancing security by protecting data in transit. This recipe will demonstrate setting up SSL authentication in PostgreSQL.

Configure PostgreSQL to Use SSL

Use OpenSSL to generate a self-signed SSL certificate and key pair:

```
openssl req -new -x509 -days 365 -nodes -out server.crt -
keyout server.key
```

Ensure the server key is not world-readable:

```
chmod 600 server.key
```

Edit the **postgresql.conf** file to enable SSL and specify the paths to the SSL certificate and key files:

```
ssl = on

ssl_cert_file = '/path/to/server.crt'

ssl_key_file = '/path/to/server.key'
```

Restart PostgreSQL to apply changes:

```
sudo systemctl restart postgresql
```

SSL Authentication

Update the **pg_hba.conf** file to require SSL for specific users or connections:

```
hostssl all all 192.168.1.0/24 md5 clientcert=1
```

This entry requires SSL connections for all users connecting from the specified IP range, with client certificates enabled. Use a PostgreSQL client like **psql** to connect with SSL:

```
psql
"postgresql://alice@192.168.1.100/adventureworks?sslmode=
require"
```

This command enforces SSL encryption for the connection, ensuring data is securely transmitted. Use PostgreSQL system views to verify SSL connections:

```
SELECT ssl, client_addr FROM pg_stat_ssl WHERE ssl =
true;
```

This query checks active SSL connections to ensure SSL is correctly configured. With this, you enhanced the security of client connections, ensuring data protection during transmission.

Recipe #3: Configure Encryption with OpenSSL

Encrypting data at rest in PostgreSQL safeguards sensitive information. Transparent Data Encryption (TDE) can be implemented using OpenSSL to encrypt database files. This recipe will demonstrate configuring encryption for PostgreSQL using OpenSSL.

Encrypt Database Files

Ensure OpenSSL is installed on your system. Then, use the following command:

```
sudo apt-get update

sudo apt-get install openssl
```

Use OpenSSL to generate a 256-bit AES encryption key:

```
openssl rand -out mykey.bin 32
```

This command creates a random encryption key and saves it to a file named **mykey.bin**. Use OpenSSL to encrypt PostgreSQL database files. For example, encrypt a specific database file:

```
openssl enc -aes-256-cbc -in
/var/lib/postgresql/data/mydb -out
/var/lib/postgresql/data/mydb.enc -pass file:mykey.bin
```

This command encrypts the **mydb** database file using AES-256 encryption and saves the output as **mydb.enc**. Update the **postgresql.conf** file to point to the encrypted database file location:

```
data_directory = '/var/lib/postgresql/data_encrypted'
```

Ensure the encrypted directory path is correctly set for PostgreSQL to access the encrypted files.

Decrypt and Access Encrypted Files

Start the PostgreSQL server and verify it uses the encrypted files:

```
sudo systemctl start postgresql
```

Use PostgreSQL queries to ensure the database is operational:

```
SELECT * FROM information_schema.tables;
```

To decrypt and access encrypted files, use OpenSSL with the appropriate key:

```
openssl enc -d -aes-256-cbc -in
/var/lib/postgresql/data/mydb.enc -out
/var/lib/postgresql/data/mydb -pass file:mykey.bin
```

This command decrypts the file, making it accessible for PostgreSQL. By configuring encryption with OpenSSL, you secured the database files, protecting sensitive data and enhancing overall data security.

Recipe #4: Implement Audit Logging with pgAudit and Triggers

Audit logging for monitoring database activities ensures compliance, and enhancing security. PostgreSQL provides auditing capabilities through extensions like pgAudit and triggers. This recipe will demonstrate implementing audit logging using both methods to capture detailed activity logs in the AdventureWorks database.

Up and Running with pgAudit

Use the PostgreSQL package manager to install pgAudit:

```
sudo apt-get install postgresql-16-pgaudit
```

This command installs the pgAudit extension for PostgreSQL 16. Connect to the database and enable the pgAudit extension:

```
CREATE EXTENSION pgaudit;
```

This command activates pgAudit for the database, allowing for detailed logging. Update the **postgresql.conf** file to configure pgAudit settings:

```
pgaudit.log = 'ddl, write'
```

This configuration logs all DDL and write operations, providing insights into changes made to the database schema and data. Restart the PostgreSQL service to apply the changes:

```
sudo systemctl restart postgresql
```

Verify pgAudit Logging

Run some SQL commands to generate audit logs:

```
INSERT INTO employees (name, position) VALUES ('John
Doe', 'Manager');

ALTER TABLE employees ADD COLUMN department VARCHAR(50);
```

Access the audit logs to review captured activities:

```
cat /var/log/postgresql/postgresql.log | grep AUDIT
```

This command filters the PostgreSQL logs to display audit entries generated by pgAudit.

Create Trigger Function

Define a table to store audit logs:

```
CREATE TABLE employees_audit (

  audit_id SERIAL PRIMARY KEY,

  change_time TIMESTAMP DEFAULT NOW(),

  user_name TEXT,

  operation TEXT,

  old_data JSONB,

  new_data JSONB

);
```

This table stores information about changes made to the **employees** table. Create a trigger function to log changes:

```
CREATE OR REPLACE FUNCTION log_employee_changes() RETURNS
TRIGGER AS $$

DECLARE

  old_data JSONB;

  new_data JSONB;

BEGIN

  IF TG_OP = 'DELETE' THEN
```

```
    old_data := row_to_json(OLD);

    INSERT INTO employees_audit (user_name, operation,
old_data)

    VALUES (current_user, TG_OP, old_data);

    RETURN OLD;

  ELSIF TG_OP = 'UPDATE' THEN

    old_data := row_to_json(OLD);

    new_data := row_to_json(NEW);

    INSERT INTO employees_audit (user_name, operation,
old_data, new_data)

    VALUES (current_user, TG_OP, old_data, new_data);

    RETURN NEW;

  ELSIF TG_OP = 'INSERT' THEN

    new_data := row_to_json(NEW);

    INSERT INTO employees_audit (user_name, operation,
new_data)

    VALUES (current_user, TG_OP, new_data);

    RETURN NEW;

  END IF;

  RETURN NULL;

END;

$$ LANGUAGE plpgsql;
```

Create a trigger for the **employees** table:

```
CREATE TRIGGER employee_audit_trigger

AFTER INSERT OR UPDATE OR DELETE ON employees

FOR EACH ROW EXECUTE FUNCTION log_employee_changes();
```

This trigger captures changes and logs them to the **employees_audit** table. Insert, update, or delete records in the **employees** table to generate audit logs:

```
UPDATE employees SET position = 'Senior Manager' WHERE
name = 'John Doe';
```

Query the **employees_audit** table to review logged activities:

```
SELECT * FROM employees_audit;
```

This query displays all logged changes, providing a detailed audit trail. By combining pgAudit and trigger-based logging, you implemented a detailed audit logging solution for the database, enhancing security and compliance capabilities.

Recipe #5: Install and Configure LDAP Authentication

LDAP (Lightweight Directory Access Protocol) authentication enables PostgreSQL to authenticate users against a centralized directory service, such as Microsoft Active Directory or OpenLDAP. This provides a secure and centralized user management system. This recipe will demonstrate setting up LDAP authentication for PostgreSQL.

Up and Running with LDAP

Install the LDAP client package on the PostgreSQL server and then use the following command:

```
sudo apt-get install ldap-utils
```

This package allows the server to communicate with the LDAP directory. Configure the LDAP client by editing **/etc/ldap/ldap.conf**:

```
BASE dc=gitforgits,dc=com

URI ldap://ldap.gitforgits.com
```

Replace **gitforgits.com** with your domain and **ldap.gitforgits.com** with the LDAP server's address. Modify the **pg_hba.conf** file to use LDAP authentication for specific users or IP ranges:

```
host    all             all             192.168.1.0/24
ldap ldapserver=ldap.gitforgits.com ldapport=389
ldapprefix="uid="
ldapsuffix=",ou=users,dc=gitforgits,dc=com"
```

This entry configures PostgreSQL to authenticate users from the specified IP range using LDAP, specifying the LDAP server and user DN format. Then, restart the PostgreSQL service to apply the changes:

```
sudo systemctl restart postgresql
```

Test LDAP Authentication

Use a PostgreSQL client like **psql** to connect with LDAP credentials:

```
psql -h localhost -U
uid=john,ou=users,dc=gitforgits,dc=com -d adventureworks
```

This command connects to the database using LDAP credentials for the user **john**. Review PostgreSQL logs to verify successful LDAP authentication:

```
tail -f /var/log/postgresql/postgresql.log
```

This command monitors the PostgreSQL logs for authentication entries, confirming LDAP integration. Ensure that your LDAP server is properly configured and that network connectivity is reliable to maintain seamless authentication.

Summary

To sum up, you learned about advanced security and authentication methods in PostgreSQL. You explored how to manage roles and authorizations, which involved creating roles and users, setting attributes, and configuring authentication methods to control access to the database. This knowledge enhanced the security of the database by ensuring that only authorized users could access sensitive data. Additionally, you discovered how to set up SSL authentication to encrypt data transmissions between clients and the server. This process involved generating SSL certificates, configuring PostgreSQL for SSL, and verifying secure connections. Implementing SSL enhanced data security by protecting against unauthorized access and interception.

The chapter also covered implementing audit logging using pgAudit and triggers, allowing you to monitor and record database activities. By configuring audit logs and setting up triggers, you gained the ability to track changes and ensure compliance with security policies. Finally, you learned how to configure LDAP authentication, which enabled PostgreSQL to authenticate users against a centralized directory service. This integration streamlined user management, reduced administrative overhead, and enhanced security by centralizing account control. Overall, Chapter 9 equipped you with essential skills for securing and managing PostgreSQL databases effectively.

CHAPTER 10: IMPLEMENTING DATABASE BACKUP STRATEGIES

Introduction

This chapter presents various strategies for implementing database backups in PostgreSQL. You will be learning how to automate database backups using shell scripts and cron jobs. This will involve creating a backup script for the database, scheduling regular backups, and ensuring that your data is consistently backed up to prevent loss due to system failures or other issues. You will be discovering how to set up continuous archiving for PostgreSQL to enable point-in-time recovery. This will include configuring your database to archive transaction logs and creating base backups. Furthermore, you will be focusing on incremental and differential backups using tools like **pgBackRest** and **pg_probackup**. These methods will enable you to capture only the changes made since the last full backup, optimizing storage use and reducing backup times. By mastering these backup strategies, you will ensure that your database is protected efficiently, balancing resource use with data security.

Finally, you will be learning how to execute schema-level backups, allowing you to selectively back up specific parts of your database. This chapter teaches bringing flexibility in managing backups to target particular schemas while saving time and storage space. By the end of this chapter, you will have strong skills of various backup techniques, ensuring robust data protection and recovery capabilities.

Recipe #1: Automate Database Backup

Automating database backups is essential for ensuring data integrity and minimizing the risk of data loss. In this recipe, you will learn how to automate the backup process for the database using a shell script and cron jobs.

Schedule the Backup with Cron

Begin by creating a shell script that utilizes the **pg_dump** utility to back up the database. Following is an example script:

```
#!/bin/bash

# Set the current date and time for the backup file name

DATE=$(date +%Y-%m-%d_%H-%M-%S)

# Define the directory where backups will be stored

BACKUP_DIR=/path/to/backup/dir
```

```
# Specify the database name

DB_NAME=adventureworks



# Path to the pg_dump utility

PG_DUMP=/usr/bin/pg_dump



# Perform the backup

$PG_DUMP -Fc $DB_NAME > $BACKUP_DIR/$DB_NAME-$DATE.dump
```

Replace **/path/to/backup/dir** with the actual path where you want to store the backup files. Change the script's permissions to make it executable:

```
chmod +x /path/to/backup/script.sh
```

This command ensures that the script can be executed from the command line. Execute the backup script manually to verify that it works correctly:

```
./path/to/backup/script.sh
```

Check the specified backup directory to confirm that a backup file with the current date and time has been created. Automate the backup process by scheduling the script to run at regular intervals using cron jobs. Edit the crontab file to schedule the backup script:

```
crontab -e
```

Add the following line to schedule the backup to run daily at midnight:

```
0 0 * * * /path/to/backup/script.sh
```

This cron job runs the backup script every day at midnight, creating a new backup file each time.

Test Backup and Restore

Ensure that the backup files are stored in a secure location to prevent unauthorized access. Consider using secure storage solutions like encrypted drives or cloud storage with strong access controls. Now, regularly test the backup and restore process to ensure that your backup files are valid and can be restored successfully. Use **pg_restore** to test the restore process:

```
pg_restore -C -d postgres /path/to/backup/file.dump
```

This command restores the backup to the specified database, allowing you to verify the integrity of the backup file. By automating database backups with a shell script and cron jobs, you ensure that the database is regularly backed up, minimizing the risk of data loss due to system failures or other issues.

Recipe #2: Execute Continuous Archiving PostgreSQL Backup

Continuous archiving allows for point-in-time recovery by continuously archiving transaction logs. This recipe will demonstrate setting up continuous archiving for the database.

Monitor WAL Archiving

Edit the **postgresql.conf** file to enable archiving:

```
archive_mode = on

archive_command = 'cp %p /path/to/backup/archive/%f'

wal_level = replica

max_wal_senders = 3

wal_keep_size = 64
```

Replace **/path/to/backup/archive** with the actual path where you want to store the archived transaction logs. Restart the PostgreSQL service to apply the changes:

```
sudo systemctl restart postgresql
```

This command restarts the PostgreSQL server with the updated configuration.

Use **pg_basebackup** to create a base backup of the database:

```
pg_basebackup -U postgres -D /path/to/backup/base -Ft -Xs
-P
```

This command creates a base backup of the database cluster, storing it in the specified directory. Execute transactions on the database to generate WAL files and verify that they are being archived correctly:

```
INSERT INTO employees (name, position) VALUES ('Alice',
'Engineer');
```

Check the archive directory to ensure that WAL files are being archived:

```
ls /path/to/backup/archive
```

Test Point-in-Time Recovery

Simulate a failure and perform a point-in-time recovery by stopping the PostgreSQL service and restoring from the base backup and WAL files:

```
sudo systemctl stop postgresql

rm -rf /var/lib/postgresql/16/main/*

cp -r /path/to/backup/base/* /var/lib/postgresql/16/main/
```

Recover the database to a specific point in time:

```
pg_restore -C -d postgres /path/to/backup/archive/
```

Start the PostgreSQL service:

```
sudo systemctl start postgresql
```

By setting up continuous archiving, you enabled point-in-time recovery for the database, ensuring holistic data protection and recovery capabilities.

Recipe #3: Working with pg_probackup and pgBackRest

pg_probackup and **pgBackRest** are advanced tools for PostgreSQL backup and recovery, offering features like incremental backups, compression, and point-in-time recovery. This recipe will instruct using these tools with the database.

Using pg_probackup

Install **pg_probackup** using the package manager:

```
sudo apt-get install pg-probackup
```

Initialize a backup directory to store backups:

```
pg_probackup init -B /path/to/backup/dir
```

This command sets up the specified directory for storing backups. Add an instance configuration for the database:

```
pg_probackup add-instance -B /path/to/backup/dir --
instance=adventureworks --
pgdata=/var/lib/postgresql/16/main
```

Create a full backup using **pg_probackup**:

```
pg_probackup backup -B /path/to/backup/dir --
instance=adventureworks --backup-mode=full --compress
```

Create an incremental backup:

```
pg_probackup backup -B /path/to/backup/dir --
instance=adventureworks --backup-mode=delta --compress
```

This command creates a backup containing only the changes since the last backup. Validate the backup integrity:

```
pg_probackup validate -B /path/to/backup/dir --
instance=adventureworks
```

This command checks the integrity of all backups for the specified instance. Restore a specific backup using its ID:

```
pg_probackup restore -B /path/to/backup/dir --
instance=adventureworks -D /var/lib/postgresql/16/main -i
backup_id
```

This command restores the specified backup to the designated data directory.

Using pgBackRest

Install **pgBackRest**:

```
sudo apt-get install pgbackrest
```

Create a configuration file for **pgBackRest**:

```
[global]

repo1-path=/path/to/backup/dir

repo1-retention-full=2

[adventureworks]

pg1-path=/var/lib/postgresql/16/main
```

Initialize the backup repository:

```
pgbackrest --stanza=adventureworks stanza-create
```

Create a full backup using **pgBackRest**:

```
pgbackrest --stanza=adventureworks --type=full backup
```

Create an incremental backup using **pgBackRest**:

```
pgbackrest --stanza=adventureworks --type=incr backup
```

This command captures changes made since the last backup, optimizing storage use and backup speed. Verify the integrity of the backups using the check command:

```
pgbackrest --stanza=adventureworks check
```

This ensures that the backups are consistent and can be restored without errors. Restore a backup with **pgBackRest**:

```
pgbackrest --stanza=adventureworks --delta restore
```

The **--delta** option applies only the changes, making the restore process faster and efficient.

Both **pg_probackup** and **pgBackRest** offer advanced backup features such as incremental and differential backups, compression, and parallel processing. These tools are suitable for enterprise environments where data integrity, storage efficiency, and backup speed are critical.

Recipe #4: Perform Incremental and Differential Backups

Incremental and differential backups are efficient strategies to capture changes made to a database since the last full backup, reducing storage requirements and backup times. This recipe will demonstrate performing incremental and differential backups using tools like **pgBackRest** and **pg_probackup**.

Incremental Backups

Begin by creating a full backup of the database using **pgBackRest**:

```
pgbackrest --stanza=adventureworks --type=full backup
```

A full backup serves as the baseline for subsequent incremental backups. Use **pgBackRest** to create an incremental backup:

```
pgbackrest --stanza=adventureworks --type=incr backup
```

Incremental backups capture only the changes made since the last backup, optimizing storage and backup speed. Restore the full backup and apply the incremental backup:

```
pgbackrest --stanza=adventureworks --type=full restore

pgbackrest --stanza=adventureworks --delta restore
```

The **--delta** option applies only the changes from the incremental backup, speeding up the restore process.

Differential Backups

Use **pg_probackup** to create a full backup of the database:

```
pg_probackup backup -B /path/to/backup/dir --
instance=adventureworks --backup-mode=full
```

Create a differential backup with **pg_probackup**:

```
pg_probackup backup -B /path/to/backup/dir --
instance=adventureworks --backup-mode=diff
```

Differential backups capture changes made since the last full backup, balancing storage efficiency and backup speed. Then, restore the full backup and apply the differential backup:

```
pg_probackup restore -B /path/to/backup/dir --
instance=adventureworks -D /var/lib/postgresql/16/main -i
backup_id
```

This process restores the full backup and applies the changes from the differential backup.

These backup strategies reduce storage requirements and improve backup efficiency. By using incremental and differential backups, you optimized the backup strategy while minimizing storage usage and backup times.

Recipe #5: Execute Schema-Level Backup

Schema-level backups allow you to selectively back up specific schemas within a database, providing flexibility and efficiency in managing backup operations. This recipe will demonstrate executing schema-level backups for the database.

Create a directory to store the schema-level backup files:

```
mkdir -p /path/to/schema/backup
```

Ensure the directory has appropriate permissions for the PostgreSQL user to write backup files.

Use the **pg_dump** utility to back up specific schemas from the database:

```
pg_dump -U postgres -h localhost -F c -b -v -f
/path/to/schema/backup/adventureworks_sales_production.ba
ckup -n sales -n production adventureworks
```

This command backs up the **sales** and **production** schemas into a compressed file. Restore the backup to a test database to verify its integrity and ensure that the schemas are present and functional:

```
pg_restore -U postgres -d testdb
/path/to/schema/backup/adventureworks_sales_production.ba
ckup
```

Execute test queries on the test database to confirm the integrity of the restored schemas:

```
SELECT * FROM sales.orders LIMIT 10;

SELECT * FROM production.products LIMIT 10;
```

By executing schema-level backups, you efficiently managed specific parts of the database, optimizing backup operations and ensuring data integrity across various database components.

Summary

To sum up, this chapter equipped you with the skills to implement various backup strategies for PostgreSQL databases. You explored automating database backups using shell scripts and cron jobs, which involved creating scripts for the database and scheduling them for regular execution. This automation ensured consistent backups and minimized data loss due to system failures. You also learned about continuous archiving to enable point-in-time recovery by configuring the database to archive transaction logs and create base backups.

Additionally, the chapter covered incremental and differential backups using tools like pgBackRest and pg_probackup, allowing you to optimize storage and reduce backup times by capturing only changes since the last full backup. Finally, you discovered how to execute schema-level backups to selectively back up specific parts of the database, providing flexibility and efficiency in backup management. These techniques equipped you with robust data protection and recovery capabilities for the database.

Chapter 11: Perform Database Recovery & Restoration

Introduction

In this chapter, you will be learning advanced database recovery and restoration techniques for PostgreSQL. You will be exploring how to perform full and point-in-time recovery (PITR) to restore databases to a previous state in the event of data loss or corruption. This includes configuring continuous archiving, creating base backups, and using WAL files to recover the database to a specific point in time. By mastering these techniques, you will enhance your ability to recover from unexpected data issues effectively.

You will also be delving into the use of Barman for advanced recovery scenarios, including tablespace and table recovery. This will involve restoring individual tablespaces or specific tables without affecting the rest of the database, providing flexibility and precision in data recovery. You will learn how to mark backups for restoration, use Barman commands for targeted recovery, and ensure data integrity through careful verification processes.

Additionally, you will focus on schema-level restoration, which allows you to recover specific schemas from backups, minimizing downtime and preserving the integrity of your database environment. This involves using Barman to restore schemas, recreating schema structures, and verifying that all objects are correctly restored. By understanding schema-level restoration, you will gain the ability to manage complex recovery scenarios with confidence.

Finally, you will be learning how to monitor restore operations using Barman, ensuring that you can track progress and troubleshoot any issues that arise during the recovery process. By leveraging Barman's monitoring capabilities, you will ensure successful and efficient data restoration, enhancing the reliability and resilience of your PostgreSQL databases.

Recipe #1: Perform Full and Point-in-Time Recovery (PITR)

Performing a full recovery or Point-in-Time Recovery (PITR) restores databases to a previous state in the event of data loss or corruption. This recipe will demonstrate both recovery processes using the database.

Full Recovery

Before starting a full recovery, make sure you have a complete backup of the database. Use **pg_dump** to create a backup if you don't have one:

```
pg_dump -U your_user -W -F t adventureworks >
adventureworks_backup.tar
```

Replace **your_user** with the appropriate PostgreSQL username. The backup will be saved as a tar file.

Remove the existing database to prepare for recovery:

```
dropdb -U your_user adventureworks
```

Recreate the database with the same name as the original:

```
createdb -U your_user adventureworks
```

Use **pg_restore** to restore the backup to the newly created database:

```
pg_restore -U your_user -d adventureworks -F t
adventureworks_backup.tar
```

After the restore process is complete, your database will be fully recovered to the state captured in the backup file.

Point-in-Time Recovery (PITR)

Enable continuous archiving in the **postgresql.conf** file:

```
wal_level = replica

archive_mode = on

archive_command = 'cp %p /path/to/archive/%f'
```

Ensure **wal_level** is set to **replica**, and adjust **archive_command** to copy WAL files to your chosen archive directory. Then, apply the configuration changes by restarting the server:

```
sudo systemctl restart postgresql
```

Use **pg_basebackup** to create a snapshot of the database:

```
pg_basebackup -U your_user -D /path/to/backup -Ft -Xs -P
```

To restore to a specific point in time, start PostgreSQL in recovery mode:

```
standby_mode = on

primary_conninfo = 'host=localhost port=5432
user=your_user'

restore_command = 'cp /path/to/archive/%f "%p"'

recovery_target_time = 'YYYY-MM-DD HH:MI:SS'
```

Create a **recovery.conf** file with these contents in the data directory and specify the target time for recovery. Then, execute the following command to start PostgreSQL in recovery mode:

```
pg_ctl start -D /path/to/data -w -t 600
```

The server will apply WAL files until it reaches the specified target time, allowing the database to be consistent at that point. Once the database reaches the target time, you can use it as usual. But, don't forget to keep WAL files secure, as they are key to the PITR process.

Recipe #2: Restore Database using Barman with Incremental/Differential Restore

Barman is a robust tool for managing PostgreSQL backups and restorations, supporting incremental and differential restores. This recipe combines restoring databases with Barman, focusing on utilizing incremental and differential backups for efficiency.

Perform Backup

To begin with, frst list the available backups for the database using Barman:

```
barman list-backup adventureworks
```

Identify the backup you wish to restore, noting the backup ID. Then, mark the selected full backup as restored to prepare for recovery:

```
barman mark-restore adventureworks full_backup_id
```

Replace **full_backup_id** with the ID of the full backup. Create a directory to store the restored database temporarily:

```
mkdir /path/to/restore
```

Restore the full backup using Barman:

```
barman recover --remote-ssh-command "ssh
user@your_server" --target-directory /path/to/restore
adventureworks full_backup_id
```

Replace **user@your_server** and **full_backup_id** with appropriate values. If an incremental or differential backup is available, mark it as restored and apply it:

```
barman mark-restore adventureworks incremental_backup_id

barman recover --remote-ssh-command "ssh
user@your_server" --target-directory /path/to/restore --
delta adventureworks incremental_backup_id
```

This process applies changes since the full backup, minimizing data restoration time.

Start PostgreSQL in Recovery Mode

Start the PostgreSQL server in recovery mode to apply archived WAL files:

```
pg_ctl -D /path/to/restore start
```

Monitor recovery progress via log files:

```
tail -f /path/to/restore/pg_log/postgresql-<date>.log
```

Once recovery is complete, stop the PostgreSQL server:

```
pg_ctl -D /path/to/restore stop
```

Synchronize the restored database with the original data directory:

```
rsync -av /path/to/restore/ /var/lib/postgresql/data/
```

Ensure ownership permissions are correct:

```
chown -R postgres:postgres /var/lib/postgresql/data/
```

Restart PostgreSQL

Restart the PostgreSQL server:

```
systemctl start postgresql
```

Connect to the restored database and verify data integrity:

```
psql -U postgres adventureworks
```

By utilizing Barman for incremental and differential restores, you enhanced the recovery process for the database, ensuring efficient data restoration with minimal downtime and storage usage.

Recipe #3: Perform Tablespace and Table Recovery

Tablespaces allow you to manage the physical storage of database objects, while individual table recovery restores specific tables without affecting the rest of the database. This recipe will demonstrate performing tablespace and table recovery using Barman for the database.

Tablespace Recovery

List the available backups for the database using Barman:

```
barman list-backup adventureworks
```

Identify the backup containing the tablespace you need to recover and note its ID. Mark the selected backup as ready for restoration:

```
barman mark-restore adventureworks backup_id
```

Replace **backup_id** with the ID of the backup you intend to restore. Create a directory to temporarily store the restored tablespace:

```
mkdir /path/to/restore
```

Use Barman to restore the tablespace:

```
barman recover-tablespace --remote-ssh-command "ssh
user@your_server" --target-directory /path/to/restore --
tablespace-name your_tablespace_name adventureworks
backup_id
```

Replace placeholders with actual values such as **your_server**, **your_tablespace_name**, and **backup_id**. Then, copy the restored tablespace to its original location on the server:

```
rsync -av /path/to/restore/
/var/lib/postgresql/data/pg_tblspc/
```

Ensure correct ownership of the tablespace directory:

```
chown -R postgres:postgres
/var/lib/postgresql/data/pg_tblspc/
```

Restart the PostgreSQL service to apply changes:

```
systemctl restart postgresql
```

Table Recovery

Check available backups for the database:

```
barman list-backup adventureworks
```

Mark the desired backup for restoration:

```
barman mark-restore adventureworks backup_id
```

Create a directory to hold the restored table:

```
mkdir /path/to/restore
```

Restore the table using Barman:

```
barman recover-table --remote-ssh-command "ssh
user@your_server" --target-directory /path/to/restore --
tablespace-name your_tablespace_name adventureworks
backup_id your_table_name
```

Fill in the placeholders such as **your_server**, **your_tablespace_name**, **backup_id**, and **your_table_name**. In the database, recreate the table structure using **psql**:

```
psql -U postgres -d adventureworks -c "CREATE TABLE
your_table_name (LIKE your_table_name INCLUDING ALL);"
```

Use **pg_restore** to load data into the new table:

```
pg_restore --data-only --table=your_table_name --
dbname=adventureworks
/path/to/restore/your_table_name.sql
```

Confirm the data restoration by querying the table:

```
psql -U postgres -d adventureworks -c "SELECT COUNT(*)
FROM your_table_name;"
```

These instructions let you use Barman to successfully perform tablespace and table recovery for the database, guaranteeing accurate data management and restoration.

Recipe #4: Perform Schema-Level Restore

A schema-level restore allows you to recover individual schemas from a backup without affecting the rest of the database, providing flexibility in managing database objects. This recipe will demonstrate performing a schema-level restore for the database using Barman.

Select and Mark Backup for Restoration

List all backups available for the database:

```
barman list-backup adventureworks
```

Identify the backup containing the schema you need to restore. Mark the backup as restored to prepare it for schema-level recovery:

```
barman mark-restore adventureworks backup_id
```

Replace **backup_id** with the ID of the backup to be restored. Set up a temporary directory to hold the restored schema:

```
mkdir /path/to/restore
```

Schema Restoration

Use Barman to recover the schema:

```
barman recover-schema --remote-ssh-command "ssh
user@your_server" --target-directory /path/to/restore --
tablespace-name your_tablespace_name adventureworks
backup_id your_schema_name
```

Replace placeholders with actual values, such as **your_server**, **your_tablespace_name**, **backup_id**, and **your_schema_name**. Create a new schema in the database using **pg_restore**:

```
pg_restore --schema-only --dbname=adventureworks
/path/to/restore/your_schema_name.sql
```

Confirm the schema restoration by listing its contents:

```
psql -U postgres -d adventureworks -c "\d
your_schema_name.*;"
```

This query verifies that all objects within the schema are restored correctly. You gained flexibility and reduced restoration downtime by performing a schema-level restore on specific database parts.

Recipe #5: Monitor Restore Operations

Monitoring restore operations ensures the success and efficiency of database recovery processes. Barman provides several tools to track the status and progress of restore operations. This recipe will demonstrate monitoring restore operations for the database using Barman.

View Restore Logs

List all restore operations for the database:

```
barman list-restore adventureworks
```

This command shows ongoing and completed restores, including their status and target directories. Then, use Barman to display the progress of a specific restore operation:

```
barman show-restore adventureworks restore_id
```

Replace **restore_id** with the ID of the restore operation you want to monitor. This displays the current status and progress, including files restored and estimated time remaining. Followed by, check the log messages for detailed information on the restore process:

```
barman show-restore-logs adventureworks restore_id
```

This command outputs log entries, providing insights into errors, warnings, or other critical events during restoration.

Verify Successful Restoration

If needed, halt a restore operation in progress:

```
barman stop-restore adventureworks restore_id
```

Stopping a restore operation removes the restore lock and cancels the ongoing process. After completion, verify the restored database by connecting and executing test queries:

```
psql -U postgres -d adventureworks
```

Conduct queries to ensure data integrity and proper functionality. You were able to observe the AdventureWorks database recovery process and guarantee effective and successful data restoration by using Barman to monitor restore operations.

Summary

All things considered, you gained knowledge of sophisticated PostgreSQL database recovery and restoration methods in this chapter. You learned setting up continuous archiving, making base backups, and utilizing WAL files to restore the database to a particular point in time in order to accomplish full and point-in-time recovery (PITR). Furthermore, you learned how to use Barman for tablespace and table recovery, enabling you to restore particular database objects without compromising the database as a whole. This required data integrity verification, backup marking, and targeted recovery with Barman commands.

Schema-level restoration was also covered in the chapter, allowing you to precisely manage complex recovery scenarios and recover individual schemas. You gained knowledge on how to replicate schema structures, validate the restoration procedure, and restore schemas using Barman. Lastly, you explored monitoring restore operations with Barman, learning how to keep tabs on developments and troubleshoot problems while the system is recovering. Overall, this chapter gave you the knowledge and abilities needed to successfully recover and restore data in PostgreSQL.

Index

W

Epilogue

Now that we've reached the end of "PostgreSQL 16 Cookbook, Second Edition," I'd like to briefly reflect about all the topics we've covered and all new areas we've explored. For me, writing this book was an eye-opening quest; I pray the same is true for you. This second edition provided an opportunity to fill any holes in the previous edition and guarantee that you have a comprehensive handbook at your fingertips, ready to face the difficulties of database management in today's fast-paced world.

In this book, we've looked into PostgreSQL 16's advanced features and capabilities, particularly the improvements in logical replication, which allow unparalleled flexibility in managing large data architectures. One of the most interesting innovations in PostgreSQL 16 is SIMD acceleration, which significantly improves data processing performance. I've showed how SIMD can revolutionize the way you manage massive datasets by incorporating realistic examples and real-world applications, allowing for faster query speeds and more efficient data processing. This functionality, combined with the improved SQL/JSON syntax, represents a considerable improvement in PostgreSQL's capabilities, and I hope you are now confident in using these approaches in your own projects.

Improved privilege management and more sophisticated authentication techniques are two ways PostgreSQL 16 demonstrates its commitment to security, an essential component of any reliable database system. I've done my best to explain these capabilities in detail so that you can protect your databases from harm while keeping them running smoothly and easily accessible. Throughout this book, I have emphasized the significance of combining PostgreSQL with current programming languages like Rust. By showing libraries such as pgx and rust-postgres, I hope to demonstrate the ability of combining PostgreSQL's rich capabilities with Rust's safety and concurrency benefits, allowing you to create efficient, scalable, and reliable database applications. As we conclude, I'd like to offer my appreciation for your dedication to learning and exploring the features of PostgreSQL 16. This book is a monument to the ongoing growth of technology and the limitless possibilities it provides. I hope it has given you useful insights, practical skills, and the confidence to innovate and excel at your job.

While this book covers a wide range of subjects and techniques, keep in mind that the world of PostgreSQL and database management is enormous and constantly changing. I encourage you to continue exploring, experimenting, and improving your knowledge. The skills and methods you've learned here are only the beginning of your journey to master PostgreSQL. Thank you for selecting "PostgreSQL 16 Cookbook, Second Edition" as your mentor. I hope it helps you on your journey as a database professional. May your future PostgreSQL projects be as fascinating and fulfilling as this one has been. Until next time, keep exploring the boundaries of PostgreSQL's capabilities.

Thank You

www.ingramcontent.com/pod-product-compliance
Lightning Source LLC
Chambersburg PA
CBHW080213170726
48282CB00030B/1106
9788119177509